100 WALKS IN
Warwickshire
& West Midlands

compiled by

IRENE BOSTON

The Crowood Press

First published in 1996 by
The Crowood Press Ltd
Ramsbury
Marlborough
Wiltshire SN8 2HR

www.crowood.com

This impression 2009

© The Crowood Press Ltd 1996

.

All rights reserved. No part of this publication may be reproduced or transmitted in
any form or by any means, electronic or mechanical, including photocopy, recording,
or any information storage and retrieval system, without permission in writing from
the publishers.

British Library Cataloguing-in-Publication Data
A catalogue record for this book is
available from the British Library

ISBN 978 1 85223 950 3

All maps by Janet Powell

Typeset by Carreg Limited, Ross-on-Wye, Herefordshire

Printed by Cromwell Press Group, Trowbridge, Wiltshire

Contents

35.	Shustoke and Nether Whitacre	5m	(8km)
36.	Harbury	5m	(8km)
37.	... and longer version	7m	(11km)
38.	Saltwells Wood and Netherton Hill	5m	(8km)
39.	Cubbington and Hunningham	5m	(8km)
40.	Long Lawford and Newbold on Avon	5m	(8km)
41.	Bulkington and Marston Jabbett	5m	(8km)
42.	Woodgate Valley	5m	(8km)
43.	Rowington	5m	(8km)
44.	Kinver Edge and Kingsford	$5^1/_2$m	(9km)
45.	Tanworth in Arden and Umberslade	$5^1/_2$m	(9km)
46.	Oversley Green and Wixford	$5^1/_2$m	(9km)
47.	Bubbenhall and Wappenbury	$5^1/_2$m	(9km)
48.	Middle Tysoe and Windmill Hill	$5^1/_2$m	(9km)
49.	Stratford-upon-Avon and Bordon Hill	6m	($9^1/_2$km)
50.	Burton Dassett and Fenny Compton	6m	($9^1/_2$km)
51.	Charlecote Park and Hampton Lucy	6m	($9^1/_2$km)
52.	Priors Marston and Priors Hardwick	6m	($9^1/_2$km)
53.	Stoneleigh and Baginton	6m	($9^1/_2$km)
54.	Lapworth and Packwood	6m	($9^1/_2$km)
55.	Wootton Wawen	6m	($9^1/_2$km)
56.	Baddesley Clinton and Wroxall	6m	($9^1/_2$km)
57.	Brailes	6m	($9^1/_2$km)
58.	Frankley and Bartley Reservoir	6m	($9^1/_2$km)
59.	The Bratch and Orton	6m	($9^1/_2$km)
60.	Waseley and Beacon Hill	6m	($9^1/_2$km)
61.	Brinklow and Easenhall	6m	($9^1/_2$km)
62.	Leamington Hastings	6m	($9^1/_2$km)
63.	Windmill End and Netherton Tunnel	6m	($9^1/_2$km)
64.	Lickey Hills and Bittell Reservoirs	$6^1/_2$m	($10^1/_2$km)
65.	Sutton Park	$6^1/_2$m	($10^1/_2$km)
66.	Henley-in-Arden	$6^1/_2$m	($10^1/_2$km)
67.	Dudley and Wrens Nest	$6^1/_2$m	($10^1/_2$km)
68.	Wilmcote and the Stratford Canal	7m	(11km)
69.	Arrow and Weethley	7m	(11km)
70.	Around Meon Hill	7m	(11km)

71.	Beaudesert and Lowsonford	7m	(11km)
72.	Womborne and Baggeridge	7m	(11km)
73.	Long Itchington and Bascote Locks	7m	(11km)
74.	Crackley Wood and Kenilworth	7^1/$_2$m	(12km)
75.	Southam and Ufton	7^1/$_2$m	(12km)
76.	Cherington and Whichford	7^1/$_2$m	(12km)
77.	Yarningale Common	7^1/$_2$m	(12km)
78.	Warmington, Ratley and Hornton	7^1/$_2$m	(12km)
79.	Caldecote and Weddington	7^1/$_2$m	(12km)
80.	Stockton and Calcutt Locks	7^1/$_2$m	(12km)
81.	Meriden and Close Wood	8m	(13km)
82.	Alvecote Pools and Polesworth	8m	(13km)
83.	Long Compton and Rollright Stones	8m	(13km)
84.	Alcester and Coughton Court	8m	(13km)
85.	Aston Cantlow and Kinwarton	8m	(13km)
86.	Fillongley	8m	(13km)
87.	Middleton	8m	(13km)
88.	Leamington and Offchurch	8m	(13km)
89.	Stourbridge Canal and Fens Pool	8m	(13km)
90.	Ullenhall	8m	(13km)
91.	Wast Hills and Weatheroak	8^1/$_2$m	(13^1/$_2$km)
92.	Coleshill and Maxstoke	8^1/$_2$m	(13^1/$_2$km)
93.	Knowle and Temple Balsall	9m	(14^1/$_2$km)
94.	Rugby and Ashlawn Cutting	9m	(14^1/$_2$km)
95.	Hay Head Wood and Barr Beacon	9^1/$_2$m	(15km)
96.	Brownhills Common and Wyrley Canal	9^1/$_2$m	(15km)
97.	Shipston-on-Stour	10m	(16km)
98.	... and longer version	12m	(19^1/$_2$km)
99.	Bidford and Welford	10m	(16km)
100.	Shuckburgh and Flecknoe	12m	(19^1/$_2$km)

PUBLISHER'S NOTE

We very much hope that you enjoy the routes presented in this book, which has been compiled with the aim of allowing you to explore the area in the best possible way - on foot.

We strongly recommend that you take the relevant map for the area, and for this reason we list the appropriate Ordnance Survey maps for each route. Whilst the details and descriptions given for each walk were accurate at time of writing, the countryside is constantly changing, and a map will be essential if, for any reason, you are unable to follow the given route. It is good practice to carry a map and use it so that you are always aware of your exact location.

We cannot be held responsible if some of the details in the route descriptions are found to be inaccurate, but should be grateful if walkers would advise us of any major alterations. Please note that whenever you are walking in the countryside you are on somebody else's land, and we must stress that you should *always* keep to established rights of way, and *never* cross fences, hedges or other boundaries unless there is a clear crossing point.

Remember the country code:

Enjoy the country and respect its life and work
Guard against all risk of fire
Fasten all gates
Keep dogs under close control
Keep to public footpaths across all farmland
Use gates and stiles to cross field boundaries
Leave all livestock, machinery and crops alone
Take your litter home
Help to keep all water clean
Protect wildlife, plants and trees
Make no unnecessary noise

The walks are listed by length - from approximately 1 to 12 miles - but the amount of time taken will depend on the fitness of the walkers and the time spent exploring any points of interest along the way. Nearly all the walks are circular and most offer recommendations for refreshments.

Good walking.

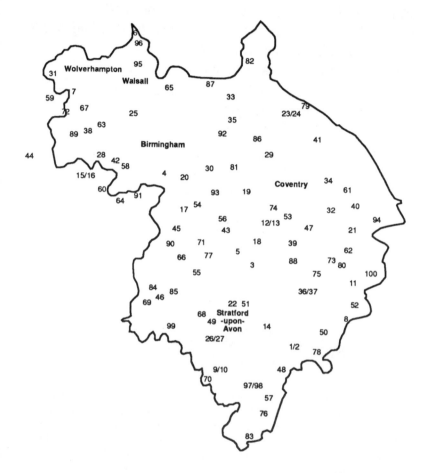

Wolverhampton
Walsall
Birmingham
Coventry
Stratford
-upon-
Avon

31
59
7
72
67
89 38 63
25
28
42 58
15/16
60
64 91
44
4
20
17 54
45
90
66
71
77
55
84 85
69 46
99
68
49
26/27
9/10
70
6
96
95
65
87
33
35
92
86
29
30 81
93 19
56
43
18
5
3
74 53
12/13
39
88
22 51
14
97/98
48
57
76
83
82
79
23/24
41
34
61
32 40
47
21
62
73 80
75
36/37
11
52
8
50
1/2
78
94
100

Walks 1 & 2   **RADWAY AND EDGE HILL** $2\frac{1}{2}$m (4km)
or 6m ($9\frac{1}{2}$km)

Maps: OS Sheets Landranger 151; Pathfinder 1021.
An undulating walk to the site of a Civil War battle, along roads, and back through delightful woodland.
Start: At 368481, Radway Church.

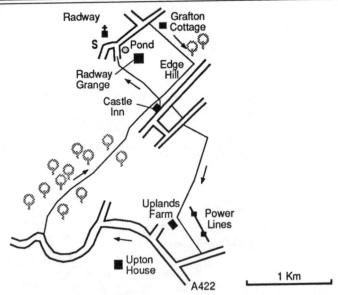

Go north-eastwards through **Radway** until just after the bus stop on the right. Now take the path in front of Grafton Cottage, going past the allotments and through a gate. Go over a stile and climb a long field towards woodland. Go through a kissing gate and ignore a Centenary Way sign on the left, turning right along a well-defined, but sometimes muddy, path, which runs along the edge of the woods, giving views of Radway Grange. Ignore all side paths to reach a major path fork.

The shorter route goes right here, out on to **Edge Hill,** continuing to a point where the longer route rejoins over a stile on the left.

The longer route goes left, along an eroded path to the Castle Inn. Turn left along the road, and just past the inn's car park and a cottage, look for a yellow arrow on the

8

right. Follow this path between buildings to reach a minor road. Almost opposite another yellow arrow points the way, going past an orchard and field. At a T-junction of paths, turn right and follow a hedge for at least a mile. The path crosses a stile and then drops sharply down a field edge with a ruined building on the left. Climb up the other side of the field, go through a waymarked gate and approach farm buildings. Now watch for a yellow arrow on the left, a path going over a stile and behind the farm buildings. This narrow path winds between trees and emerges by power lines into a field. Continue to reach a minor road. Turn right to reach a T-junction. Go right, with care, along the busy A422, using the grass verge for a mile and passing **Upton House**. Ignore two side roads, and at the top of a steep hill watch for a gap on the right. Although not waymarked, this path carries the Centenary Way. It can be overgrown at first, but soon becomes clearer. Follow the path for over a mile, passing Edgehill Farm on the right and across a lane, the path continuing just past a telegraph pole. Cross another lane and go up steps by a line of beech trees. At the next set of steps, with a Centenary Way marker, go down left and follow the path as it descends to the edge of a wood. Go over a stile to rejoin the shorter route.

Drop down across open fields with views to Radway House and the Civil War Battlefield (not accessible) in a field on the right. At the bottom of the hill go through a gate on to the lane, turning right past the village pond to emerge onto the road by Radway Church.

POINTS OF INTEREST:

Radway – This charming village has a 19th-century chapel, built on a new site in 1866. Sanderson Miller, the squire of Radway, was one of the pioneers of Gothic architecture and made considerable alterations to Radway Grange. He also built Edgehill Tower, now the Castle Inn, which stands on the alleged site where Charles I's standard was raised on the eve of battle.

Edge Hill – A wonderful viewpoint across Warwickshire. The battle site is owned by the MoD and not open to the public. The battle, on 23rd October, 1642, between the Royalists and the Parliamentarians proved inconclusive although both sides suffered heavy casualties. The hilltop site looked very different then, being bare of trees.

Upton House – This National Trust property has magnificent collections of porcelain and paintings. The lovely gardens, full of mature trees and splendid floral displays, are well worth exploring. Set on different levels, the full sweep of the gardens is not revealed until you step almost to the edge of the lawn.

REFRESHMENTS:
The Castle Inn, Edgehill.

Walk 3   **WARWICK: TOWN AND CASTLE**   3m (5km)

Maps: OS Sheets Landranger 151; Pathfinder 976

Exploring a fascinating town, steeped in history, and a fine castle.

Start: At 287648, St Nicholas car park, Castle Bridge.

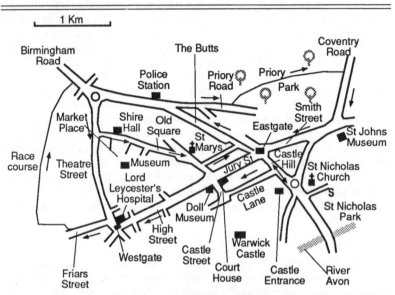

Cross the main road, with care, and turn left, to the bridge, for a stunning view of the castle. Retrace your steps past the car park entrance to reach Mill Street, beyond which is an entrance to **Warwick Castle**; allow at least three hours for a thorough exploration. Return to the same entrance and go left. Turn left again up Castle Lane and right up Castle Street, passing the Doll Museum and the Court House. The latter contains the Warwickshire Town and Yeomanry Museums, as well as the Tourist Information Centre. Jury Street (once known as Jewry Street) on the right was where the Jewish population lived and worked. Turn left up High Street, passing Lord Leycester's Hospital which was formerly the Guildhall. In 1571, it became the property of Robert Dudley, Earl of Leicester, and was converted into almshouses for old soldiers; they still serve that purpose today. Walk through Westgate, above which is a 14th-century chapel. The old pillar-boxes here and in Eastgate date from 1856 and have the original vertical slots. Turn right into Theatre Street and left down Friars

Street, at the end of which is Warwick racecourse. Provided a race is not in progress, cross to the centre of the course and turn right, walking parallel with the railings and a golf course on the left. At the first bend, go under the railings to reach a stile, passing behind houses to emerge onto the Birmingham road.

Turn right and cross at the traffic lights, bearing right at a roundabout into Theatre Street. Turn left by the Shire Hall into the Market Place. Opposite is the County Museum which houses the great Sheldon tapestry map of Warwickshire. Go along Old Square heading for **St Mary's Church**, passing Northgate Street on the left. By the War Memorial, walk down the alleyway on the left, alongside the churchyard, to emerge into the Butts. Turn left to the Police Station. Turn right to enter Priory Park and keep right along the main path across the park to emerge on to Coventry road. Turn right to reach the **St John's Museum** of costume and folk life. This was the site of a hospital, dating from Henry II's reign, which gave lodgings and refreshment to poor travellers. In the 17th century the Stoughton family erected the present building. Turn right along Smith Street and left by Eastgate: the St Peter's Chapel above is part of King's High school. Now go down Castle Hill to the car park.

POINTS OF INTEREST:

Warwick Castle – Ethelfleda, daughter of King Alfred fortified the original settlement in 914. The castle was sacked during the Barons' war with Henry III in the 13th century. It then passed to the Beauchamp family who embarked on lavish rebuilding. After the death of the Earl of Warwick (the Kingmaker), the castle passed to the Crown, then to Ambrose Dudley, brother of the Queen's favourite Robert Dudley, and on to Sir Fulke Greville. In 1642 the castle survived a siege by Royalists and was sold by the present Earl in 1978 to Madame Tussaud's.

St Mary's Church – As magnificent as any cathedral, the church is a landmark for miles around. In the Chapter House is the tomb of Fulke Greville, whose ghost is said to haunt Watergate Tower in the castle. Alabaster tombs commemorate Thomas Beauchamp, a Commander at the Battle of Crecy in 1346, and his wife Katherine. The magnificent Beauchamp chapel contains an ornate effigy of Richard, Earl of Warwick. In the north transept is the Regimental Chapel of the Royal Warwickshire Regiment with the old colours, including the garter banner of Field Marshal Montgomery.

The church is only one of many beautiful buildings in Warwick. The town was substantially rebuilt after its own Great Fire of 1694.

REFRESHMENTS:

There are endless possibilities, to suit all tastes, in Warwick.

Walk 4   **SAREHOLE MILL**   3m (5km)

Maps: OS Sheets Landranger 139; Pathfinder 934 and 954. The Birmingham A-Z is also useful.

A delightful, easy walk alongside the River Cole and around Trittiford Mill pool.

Start: At 099818, the Recreation Ground car park.

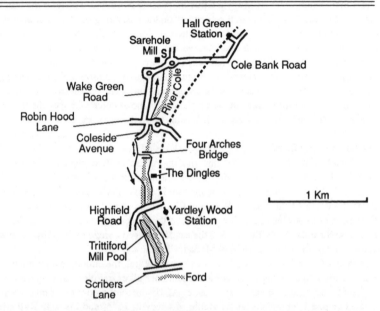

Turn right along the road past **Sarehole Mill** to reach a gravel path opposite the car park. This path runs alongside the **River Cole**, with Wake Green Road over to the right. On reaching Robin Hood Lane, cross to Coleside Avenue, at the end of which, walk past Four Arches Bridge on the left (this is part of the return route). Go past trees, to the left, and past another bridge, then walk down an avenue of trees. Cross an open green area and go over a footbridge on the left.

Turn right, with water on both sides. This is where, in the 18th century, a mill race was built which increased the water supply to Sarehole Mill. Follow the path leads to Highfield Road. Cross to the grass, continuing to Trittiford Mill pool, which is rich in birdlife. Walk around the pool, through Trittiford Mill Park, skirting Scriber's Lane at the end of the pool. The ford off to the right is well worth a visit, retaining a surprisingly rural feel considering it is in the middle of an urban area.

After completing the circuit of the pool, you will arrive back at Highfield Road. Take the path to the right of the river. This leads through a narrow green area known as the Dingles and eventually reaches Four Arches Bridge where you rejoin the outward path. This can be reversed, but an alternative return route from Trittiford Mill pool is to catch the train from Yardley Wood station to Hall Green. From Hall Green station, turn right to Cole Bank Road, where another right turn will take you back to Sarehole Mill.

POINTS OF INTEREST:

Sarehole Mill – It is believed that a water mill has stood on this site since the Middle Ages, but the present, restored, mill buildings date from the 18th century. The mill is one of only a few remaining out of the 70 which once operated in the Birmingham area, six in the Hall Green area alone. The mill ceased commercial operations in 1919 and the building was allowed to deteriorate. Restored to working order in the 1960's, it opened as a museum in 1969 and houses a fascinating display of old pictures and tools which illustrate the mill's history. At the present time, it is open from early April to the end of October, from 2.00 – 5.00pm each day but it would be best to ring and check (tel: 0121 777 6612).

The area has several associations with famous people. As a child J R R Tolkien, author of *The Hobbit* and *The Lord of the Rings* lived nearby, in what is now Wake Green Road, and the late TV comedian Tony Hancock was born at 41 Southam Road, where a commemorative plaque can be seen on the wall.

River Cole – The river threads its way through the industrial suburbs of Birmingham and is being promoted by the City Council as a valuable walkway.

REFRESHMENTS:

There are a cafe and an inn in Highfield Road.

Walk 5　　　　　　**HATTON LOCKS**　　　　　$3^1/_2$m ($5^1/_2$km)

Maps: OS Sheets Landranger 151; Pathfinder 976.

An interesting canal with fine views to Warwick, returning across fields and the railway. Some muddy paths.

Start: At 244669, Hatton Locks car park.

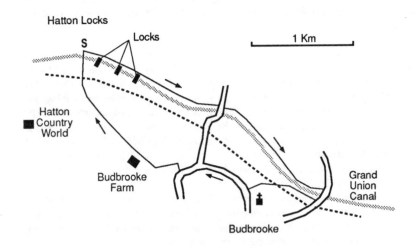

Walk left along the towpath of the **Grand Union Canal**, in the direction of Warwick, with good views across **Hatton Locks** towards St Mary's Church, Warwick. The path can be muddy as it passes under two bridges (Numbers 53 and 52). After $1^1/_2$ miles, the canal swings left: just before the next bridge take the path which climbs up on to the road. Turn right over the canal bridge and follow the minor road for 100 yards to reach a gate. Go through to reach a footbridge and follow the arrows around the left edge of the field, parallel to the railway. Go under a bridge, through a gate and turn right, aiming for the church at Budbrooke. Go over a stile and cross the meadow beyond to a stile and a gate leading into St Michael's Churchyard. The first path on the right leads through a gate on to a minor road in **Budbrooke.** Turn right and follow the road for $\frac{1}{2}$ mile, and then go left down a minor road signed to Hampton on the Hill. At the first bend, take the farm drive on the right towards Budbrooke Farm.

The drive swings left, then right in front of farm buildings: at the next bend, watch for a yellow arrow by a gate on the right. Go through the gate and cross a field to the stile ahead. After wet weather this path can be a quagmire and muddy feet are guaranteed. Those who reach the stile first can relish their companions floundering in the mud behind them! Cross the stile and bear half-right across a field to reach a metal footbridge. Cross and climb up into the next field, where the path is well waymarked. At a gap in the hedge, aim across a field on a good headland towards the railway line. A sign just before the stile is a reminder that there is no access to **Hatton Country World** from this direction. Go over the stile, cross the railway line, with care, and descend the bank. Go over a stile into Brooks Marsh, a conservation area and part of the Country World Nature Trail. Cross the field and climb the last stile to emerge by Hatton Locks. The car park lies over the canal bridge. If a visit to Hatton Country World is desired, after climbing the last stile, turn left along the towpath, going past the top lock and the lock keeper's cottage to reach St John's Bridge, where another left turn along the road will bring you to the centre.

POINTS OF INTEREST:

Grand Union Canal – Formed in 1929, the Canal is an amalgamation of several waterways and runs for 137 miles from Birmingham to the Thames. The 1930s saw improvements, including the widening of the narrow locks, each lock contains some 50,000 gallons of water. The remains of the old locks are used as overflows.

Hatton Locks – Also known as Hatton Flight or Stairway to Heaven, this is a series of 21 locks taking the Grand Union Canal down into the Avon valley, descending 146 feet in two miles. It was originally part of the Birmingham and Warwickshire Canal. Construction began in 1793 and was completed in 1800. It became part of the Grand Union Canal in 1929, and was officially opened by the Duke of Kent in 1934.

Budbrooke – The site of a medieval village, the partly Norman church of St Michael's having a distinctive 13th-century tower. It was the garrison church for the Royal Warwickshire Regiment, although the barracks in the village closed in 1960. The regimental colours hang on the north wall.

Hatton Country World – The 19th-century farm buildings are now a collection of craft workshops and a 20 acre farm park with a pets' corner and nature trails.

REFRESHMENTS:

The Waterman Inn – reached by a path at the back of the Hatton Locks car park.

Walk 6   **CHASEWATER**   3¹/₂m (5¹/₂km)

Maps: OS Sheets Landranger 128 and 139; Pathfinder 892.
A marvellous walk around a reservoir and across heathland.
Plenty of interest for nature lovers.
Start: At 036072, Chasewater car park.

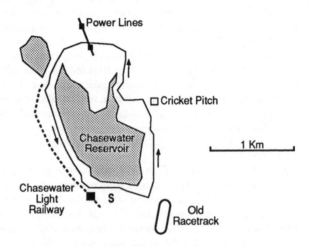

Return to the car park entrance with the reservoir on your left, and turn left up the
lane. Walk over a bridge and past a pool on the right to join a path along the top of
Chasewater dam. Follow the path, with good views over the reservoir, until it drops
to rejoin the road by a junction. Go down the lane on the left, and, at a left bend, take
the path on the right, going through heathland to reach a stile by a cricket pitch and a
junction of paths. Take the left-hand path which winds through trees to emerge on to
grass by the reservoir. Turn right, and then shortly left along another well-worn path
which follows the water's edge, and then goes alongside an isolated arm of the reservoir.

    Turn left across the head of the pool and up a steep path, at the top of which you
can see across the whole expanse of heathland. Any of the paths at this quieter northern
end of the reservoir are worth exploring, having much to interest birdwatchers and

botanists. To continue the walk, keep ahead along the main path and then bear left at a fork. Go ahead across a junction of tracks and downhill to another path junction. Now take the middle track, with a hedge on the right, heading towards a line of pylons. Where the path becomes enclosed on both sides, turn right up a steep bank and then left along a track above the line of a dismantled railway.

Go past a pool and the remains of old railway sleepers, and then drop down to walk along a path by the **Chasewater Light Railway** track. Cross the causeway between the pools and at its end turn left along a wide path, with good views over the reservoir, now on your left. Continue to reach open ground near the railway station. Now turn left along the tarmac lane or the water's edge to reach the car park.

POINTS OF INTEREST:

Chasewater – This is the largest area of open water in the Midlands. It was built in 1844 as a feeder reservoir to supply water to the Birmingham canal system and is now a popular venue for watersports, becoming very busy in summer. It is much quieter in the winter months and at this time, and during migration periods, the birdwatcher will be richly rewarded. Up to 200 different species of birds have been recorded here and the reservoir is an important stopover for migrants, particularly waders. The reservoir is also very important for wintering birds, in particular a huge gull roost which may comprise as many as 15,000 birds. Many rare plants and insects, including orchids, sundews and rare heathers, thrive on the fragments of heathland and areas of wetland to the north.The derelict grandstand near the entrance of the car park once overlooked the Chasewater raceway, a trotting track in use until 1984.

Chasewater Light Railway – Chasewater steam railway, based at the old Brownhills west station, runs along the track of the old Cannock Chase and Wolverhampton railway.

REFRESHMENTS:

There is a cafe at the Chasewater Light Railway, and a kiosk/cafe in Chasewater Park.

Walk 7   PENN AND GOSPEL END   3¹/₂m (5¹/₂km)

Maps: OS Sheets Landranger 139; Pathfinder 912.

Easy walking around Penn Common and across fields.

Start: At 895954, Penn Church.

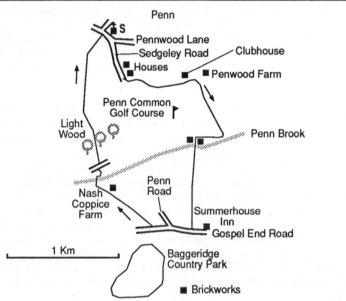

From the church on Church Hill, turn left down Pennwood Lane. Shortly, turn right down Sedgley Road. Walk downhill towards **Penn Common** and, where the houses end, turn left along a track. Just by a gateway, turn off the track and walk beside the hedge which borders the golf course on Penn Common. Head towards the clubhouse and go through the car park beyond the building. Just before Penwood Farm, turn right on a path which leads through trees and then goes downhill along the edge of the golf course. Just before reaching Penn Brook, turn half-right and head towards a house. Walk past the house, but before the next house, go left over a stile. Cross a footbridge over Penn Brook and climb the bank to go over a stile. Maintain direction across two fields, linked by stiles, with Baggeridge brickworks seen ahead.

In the third field, walk ahead to reach a gap between houses. Go through on to Gospel End road. The inn is along the road to the left, but the route turns right, then crosses Penn Road. Just opposite the entrance to **Baggeridge Country Park,** cross a stile on the right and follow the hedge on the right around the field to reach a gate. Go through and head half-left across three fields, linked by stiles. Eventually you drop down to Penn Brook, passing Nash Coppice Farm, off to the right. Cross a footbridge and bear slightly right to reach a stile by a gate.

Go over and follow the path beyond to a road. Cross and follow a path across the golf course, but on the opposite side of the course from that passed earlier. The path bears left, then right towards the woodland of Light Wood. Go over a track and follow the hedge on the left to a junction. Take the bridleway ahead and walk beside the hedge up the side of the old track. The path leads to a field and bears half right across it to reach Penn Church and the start.

POINTS OF INTEREST:
Penn Common – The village of Penn is set high, with superb views to Shropshire and the hills of Birmingham. The preaching cross is said to have been erected by Leofric and his wife, Lady Godiva.
Baggeridge Country Park – The Parkland was once part of the Himley Hall estate. Coal production ceased in 1968 and it was designated a Country Park in 1970. Reclamation work, including the planting of 20,000 trees and shrubs, was completed over the next decade, with the park opening in 1983. Whites Wood has sycamore and birch and, in the Spring, bluebells, wood anemones and wood sorrel thrive. The pools were created in the mid-18th century. Fragile heath and grassland support many species of butterfly, including Meadow Brown, Gatekeeper and Small Heath.

REFRESHMENTS:
The Old Stag's Head, Penn.
The Summerhouse, Gospel End.

Walk 8 **Wormleighton and the Oxford canal**   4m (6$\frac{1}{2}$km)
Maps: OS Sheets Landranger 151; Pathfinder 999.
*A delightful ramble through a quiet village and alongside a canal,
returning across fields. Some muddy paths.*
Start: At 448536, the Gatehouse, Wormleighton.

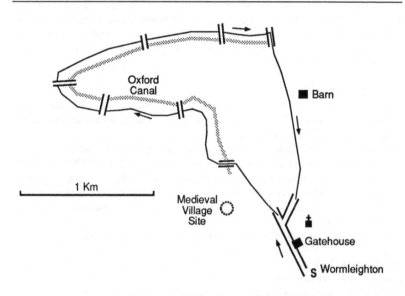

Walk under the gatehouse in **Wormleighton** and along the lane towards St Peter's
Church. Almost opposite the church is a lane on the left, marked with a yellow arrow:
walk down this and at the bottom pass the old village fishponds on the right. Go over
a stile and climb the bank in front to reveal the way ahead. The path aims for the canal
bridge at the far end of the field. The disconcerting sight of canal boats which seem to
drift along amid the hedgerows is a good guide. As you cross the field, look for the
ridges and furrows marking the site of the old village. Go through a handgate in the
top right-hand corner of the field and cross the bridge.

The path descends the left hand-side of the bridge: the right hand side can be
overgrown. Turn left under the bridge, and follow the **Oxford Canal** towpath as it
swings in large curves through the countryside, giving good views for the next

$2^1/_2$ miles. The towpath has been reinforced in places and provides a solid surface of cemented sandbags where the original bank has worn away, but great care is needed if the conditions are muddy. Along the way you pass five canal bridges, one of which seems to be made from the trunk of a single tree. The canal bustles with many pleasure boats during the summer.

At the sixth bridge, Number 128, leave the towpath to turn right, over the bridge on to a bridleway which climbs gradually through fields. As you climb, a marvellous view opens out behind across North Warwickshire. After passing a barn on the left, and at the top of the slope, the track becomes a tarmac lane: continue along it, passing houses to emerge into the village by the church seen earlier. Go back under the gatehouse to return to the start of the walk.

POINTS OF INTEREST:

Wormleighton – The splendid gatehouse dates from 1613 and is adorned with the coat of arms of the Spencer family. The old village, called "Old Towne" on a 1634 map in the church, had cottages, a manor house and fishponds, but was depopulated by famine, plague and the sheep enclosures. It was finally destroyed in 1498 by William Cope, a prosperous sheep farmer. In 1506 John Spencer built the new manor house, which became the centre of a vast estate. At the same time he acquired Althorp in Northamptonshire and was a distant ancestor of the current Spencer family. The manor house, of which only a fragment now remains, was used as a base by Prince Rupert, King Charles' nephew, in the Civil War, and was destroyed by Royalists to stop it falling into the hands of the Parliamentarians. The fine 13th-century St Peter's Church has a perpendicular rood screen and loft, Jacobean panelling, tiles, fragments of mediaeval stained glass and a wall monument to John Spencer dated 1610.

Oxford Canal – The canal is one of a series of waterways conceived by James Brindley. This section was finished in 1778 and links with the Grand Union canal further north.

REFRESHMENTS:

None on the route or in Wormleighton. The nearest is the *George and Dragon*, on the A423 near Fenny Compton.

Maps: OS Sheets Landranger 151; Pathfinder 1020 and 1021.
*A fairly strenuous walk from a charming village, with glorious
views and a longer option.*
Start: At 210433, the village green, Ilmington.

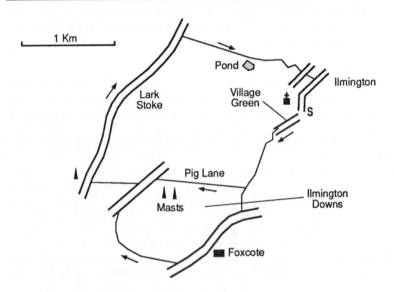

With the war memorial on your right, continue up the narrow road, past houses, to reach a fork in the path. Go over a stile on the right and turn left to follow a well-marked, but sometimes muddy, path to another stile. Go over, turn left and climb along the edge of the field. The views open out behind as height is gained and are an excellent excuse to pause for breath. There is no need to negotiate the first stile you reach – the fence has been removed! However, you must go over the next stile: continue the climb to reach a T-junction of paths on top of **Ilmington Downs**.

The shorter route turns right here, going along a bridleway known as Pig Lane, with marvellous views stretching across three counties. After ¹/₂ mile, you pass two masts on the left: drop down to a road where the longer option rejoins the route.

The longer route goes straight on, downhill, along the field edge, to join a lane leading to Foxcote House. Turn right and walk along the drive. Just before the house, watch for a yellow waymark on the fence. Do not enter the driveway: instead, walk beside the hedge, ignoring a lane on the right. Climb past the next farmhouse and look for a yellow arrow on a gate, ignoring a blue arrow pointing straight ahead. Cross a field to reach a gate, and keep beside the left edge of the next field to reach another gate. Now switch to the right edge of a long field, eventually emerging on to a lane. Turn right, past houses, to rejoin the shorter route at gate on the left.

Go through a handgate (no waymark) on the opposite side of the lane and climb to reach another gate in the top right corner of a field. The path now hugs the field edge, going straight on to reach a minor road near another mast. On a clear day the views ahead are of the Malverns. Turn right and descend the lane, for nearly a mile, to reach the second turning on the right. Go through the gateway and watch for a Centenary Way sign on the left. Descend beside the field, cross a stile and a stream and climb the slope to another stile. Continue with a hedge on your right: most of the gates have been removed making it unnecessary to climb the next stile. Ignore another stile on the right with a profusion of waymarking, but cross the next stile into a field on the right. Continue, on the same line, across three fields to emerge into **Ilmington** by the side of a school. Turn right, and almost immediately left, into another field with a large pond at the far end. Pass to the left of the pond and go through two more gates into an alleyway by a stream which runs through the centre of the village. Turn right, and when you emerge into another lane, watch for the continuation of the alleyway which eventually leads to St Mary's Church. Turn left to reach the village green.

POINTS OF INTEREST:
Ilmington Downs – The Downs are on the northernmost spur of the Cotswolds and offer wonderful walking with rolling hills, well-marked paths and spectacular views. Pig Lane, which crosses the Downs, is an ancient route, possibly of Roman origin. It is said to derive its name from the pigs which were once driven along it.
Ilmington Village – A fascinating village, with cottages almost Cotswold in character. The traditional craft of hurdle making is still practised at a workshop in the village. St Mary's Church dates from Norman times and has an ancient sundial on the south wall of the tower. Look out for the carved mouse on the interior woodwork, which is the 'signature' of the famous woodcarver, Robert Thompson of Kilburn in Yorkshire.

REFRESHMENTS:
The Howard Arms , Ilmington.
The Red Lion, Ilmington.

Walk 11   **NAPTON ON THE HILL**   4m (6$\frac{1}{2}$km)

Maps: OS Sheets Landranger 151; Pathfinder 977 and 999.

An interesting walk past a windmill, with good views, varied scenery and wildlife along canal.

Start: At 466616, in Napton village.

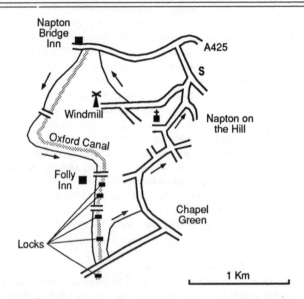

To find the start, drive along the A425 from Southam, past the Napton Bridge Inn. At the next crossroads, turn right into **Napton** village and park with consideration in the village streets. (There is no parking available at the church, other than when attending a service).

To begin, climb the road towards **St Lawrence's Church**, opposite the Crown Inn, and go over a crossroads with a sign to School Hill, passing the church on the left. The windmill soon comes into view ahead: it is now in private ownership and is not accessible. A short way along the lane towards the windmill, and just after a minor lane joins on the left, watch for a stile on the right. Go over and follow the path beyond to another stile. Go over and continue along the path to reach a fork. Go half-left, crossing stiles and then dropping downhill to reach the A425.

Turn left, with care, very shortly going over a canal bridge, (Number 111) to reach the Napton Bridge Inn. Opposite the inn, turn left to descend on to the **Oxford Canal** towpath. Turn right along the towpath, (care is needed if the conditions are wet), and follow it for 2 miles, passing three canal bridges, the Folly Inn and four canal locks along the way. At the first bridge, on the opposite side, is a modern industrial estate which stands on the site of the old Brick and Tile Works. On reaching the fourth bridge (Number 115), just before the fifth lock, go to the far side of the bridge and climb up on to a road.

Turn right, eastwards, and, shortly after, turn left through a gate, marked with a yellow arrow. Walk diagonally across the field beyond, passing the corner of two hedged fields on the right. Cross a stream over a metal bridge and climb the slope ahead to reach a stile on to a drive, by a garage. Turn left to reach a minor road at Chapel Green, which was possibly the site of a Saxon village. Turn left up the road back into Napton village and the start of the walk.

POINTS OF INTEREST:
Napton on the Hill – Built on the slopes of Napton Hill, and dominated by the church and windmill, this was already a substantial settlement by 1086. Following the grant of a weekly market and annual fair in 1321, it became a prosperous village in the Middle Ages. Napton Windmill, visible for miles around, can be traced back to 1543 and is now a private house and not open to the public. There is a mixture of architectural styles in the village's cottages and houses.
St Lawrence's Church – The church is on a fine hilltop site and dates from Norman times. Local legend has it that it was to have been built at the foot of the hill but the stones were mysteriously moved to the top of the hill overnight. The north door was known as the Devil's Door: the door was opened during Baptisms to allow the Devil to escape. There is an unusual vestry door with a hatch and grille. The restoration of the church in Victorian times was carried out by the Shuckburgh family, from nearby Shuckburgh Hall.
Oxford Canal – Designed by James Brindley, the canal links with the Grand Union canal a few miles north. This whole section is very popular with pleasure craft.

REFRESHMENTS:
The Crown Inn, Napton.
The Folly Inn, Napton.
The Napton Bridge Inn, on the walk.

Walks 12 & 13   **KENILWORTH CASTLE**   4m (6¹/₂km)
or 6m (9¹/₂km)

Maps: OS Sheets Landranger 140 and 139; Pathfinder 955.
*An easy walk from the majestic ruined castle: across fields,
returning through woods.*
Start: At 280720, Kenilworth Castle car park.

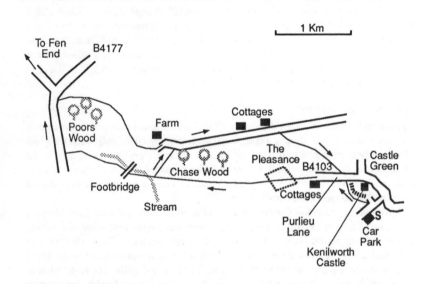

From the car park, take the path to the left of the **castle** approach. Go through a gate
and follow the path under the castle walls to reach Purlieu Lane. Turn left. Most of the
route is well maintained and waymarked, due, in part, to the efforts of the Kenilworth
Footpath Preservation Group. After passing houses, the path turns right, in front of
the last house. Here, the path can be overgrown in summer, but soon emerges into
open pasture, taking you through the site of **The Pleasance** and on to a stile in the top
left corner. Go over and walk with a hedge on your left to reach another stile. Go over
and follow the right-hand field edge. Go across a footbridge and stile to a line of trees.
Maintain direction through a long field and then cross a farm track.

    The shorter route turns right here, climbing past a wood to reach a lane.

26

The longer route maintains direction, with a hedge on the right. At the next field corner, cross a footbridge, partly hidden in trees on the left, then ignore the path straight on, turning right to follow a (sometimes indistinct) path which twists and turns along the edge of the field. Ignore an opening on the right and cross into the next field, keeping the hedge on your right. Where the hedge ends, aim across the field to reach a gap in the hedge to the right of a cottage. Go through on to a busy road. Turn right and, with care, go along the grass verges. Go past a right-hand bend and a road to Fen End, and then take a bridleway on the right. Just inside the gate is a sign "No Bad Language and No Litter!" The path can be overgrown here, which might explain the bad language! The path soon improves, passing through the beautiful Poors Wood to reach a field. Follow the right-hand edge and then turn left along a farm track. Just before the silos, turn right along a narrow path to join a tarmac lane. The first turning on the right is where the shorter route is rejoined.

Go eastwards along the road until you pass a second group of cottages, where paths goes off left and right. Take the right-hand path, going over a stile and following the well-defined path beyond, aiming for the castle in the distance. After crossing two more stiles, turn left, then go over another stile into a large field. Cross diagonally to reach a stile. At the end of the next field, go through a gate and cross a final field to reach Purlieu Lane. Turn left to reach the castle walls and the start.

POINTS OF INTEREST:
Kenilworth Castle – The castle is now in the care of English Heritage. The original building was begun by Geoffrey de Clinton in the 12th century, the keep being added by Henry II. King John enlarged the castle and it was then granted to the De Montforts. When the family rebelled against Henry III, the castle was besieged, surrendering after six months. It was visited by Queen Elizabeth when it was owned by one of her favourites, Robert Dudley, Earl of Leicester. A century later it was reduced to ruins following an attack by the Parliamentarians in the Civil War. The castle passed to Lawrence Hyde, a supporter of Charles II, whose son became Lord Clarendon. It stayed in the Clarendon family until 1937 when it was bought by Sir John Siddeley who gave it to the Office of Works. There is much left standing, including the massive keep and the Great Hall built by John of Gaunt.
The Pleasance – After draining part of the lake which surrounded the castle on three sides, Henry V built a summer house on this site in the early 15th century.

REFRESHMENTS:
The Queen and Castle Inn, Castle Green, Kenilworth.
The Clarendon Arms, Castle Green, Kenilworth.

Walk 14   COMPTON VERNEY LAKES   4m (6$^1/_2$km)
Maps: OS Sheets Landranger 151; Pathfinder 998.
A walk around two lakes (good for wildfowl) and through
beautiful parkland. Some muddy paths.
Start: At 307517, Combroke Church.

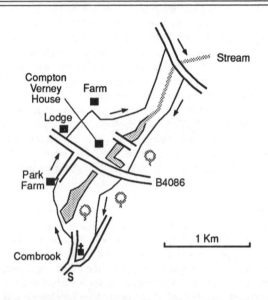

Walk along the 'No Through Road' to the left of St Mary and St Margaret's Church,
going past houses and an interesting covered well. Turn left along a narrow, signed
path by a row of cottages. Go over a brook and climb the sometimes muddy path up a
slope to a gate. Cross a field to reach a path which enters the woodland, with the lake
on the right. This path can be very muddy and soggy feet are almost guaranteed. The
lakes, as well as being excellent for bird life, are popular with fishermen. Follow the
path as it winds around the lake, going through another gate and across a field. Still
keeping the lake on your right, go through a metal gate and follow a bridleway to a
farm drive. The path is waymarked to the right of the driveway: go through a gate and
on to Park Farm drive, which passes through parkland to reach the busy B4086. Turn
left and walk up the hill on the grass verge. On drawing level with a driveway on the

28

right, cross the road, with care, and go past Compton Verney Lodge. Walk down the drive, ignoring all side turnings. Just before the farm buildings, turn right, through a gate, and walk downhill. At a fork in the track, bear left. There are good views of **Compton Verney** house and the parkland surrounding the mansion over to the right. In about a mile you reach a minor road: turn right, and after crossing a bridge, turn immediately right and walk along the edge of a field, by a stream. Keep beside the stream to reach the bridge, designed by Robert Adam, in front of Compton Verney House. The house and bridge itself are strictly private. Turn left along the drive, which winds through magnificent Redwoods, with the lake on the right, to emerge on to the B4086. Turn right, with care, and watch for the sometimes indistinct path on the left which crosses the centre of a field towards woodland. If the path is unclear, aim for a gap several hundred yards in from the right-hand edge of the wood, although this opening can be difficult to spot until you are close to the trees. Go into the woods and ignore all side tracks, maintaining direction past fenced-off areas, until the path bends sharply left. Ignore another path which goes straight on, following the left-hand path to a minor road. Turn right and follow the road downhill into **Combroke** village. The church and starting point are on the right as you enter the village.

POINTS OF INTEREST:
Compton Verney – The site appears in the Domesday Book and was granted to Robert Murdak by the Earl of Warwick. In 1370 it was given to Alice Perrers, mistress of Edward III, and in 1440 the land was possessed by Richard Verney who built the first house. The name of Compton Verney first appears in records around 1445. In 1540 Sir William Verney enlarged the property, but the mansion seen today was largely built by Vanburgh and Robert Adam in the 18th century. The house remained in the Verney family until 1921. It has now been converted into private apartments. The stretch of water which forms the two lakes was created by Capability Brown: it is now divided by the B4086 road. The magnificent bridge was designed by Robert Adam.
Combroke village – This charming, quiet village has a stream flowing through its centre into the River Dene. The church of St Mary and St Margaret has an unusual steeple and an elaborately carved doorway. The interior contains beautiful stained glass windows and a detailed architect's drawing of the church.

REFRESHMENTS:
None on the route. The nearest are in Kineton, two miles south-east.

Walks 15 & 16   **THE CLENT HILLS**   4m (6½km)
                                                 or 6m (9½km)
Maps: OS Sheets Landranger 139; Pathfinder 933 and 953.
*Exhilarating walking across wooded ridges, with glorious views
and visiting two fascinating churches.*
Start: At 937807, Nimmings car park.

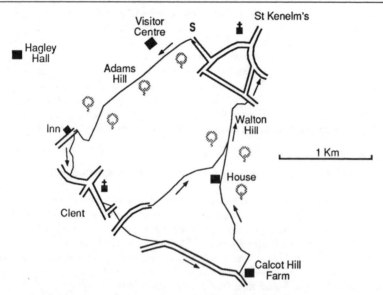

Turn right from the car park and, shortly, go through a wooden barrier on the right.
The path beyond climbs steeply through beech trees to reach the open ridge. Go along
the ridge, ignoring all side tracks, to reach the summit of Adam's Hill, in the **Clent Hills
Country Park**, with its toposcope and the Four Stones. The views from the summit,
at just over 900 feet (304m), are superb, stretching across the Midlands to the Welsh
Hills and the Malverns. Continue along the main path, passing another viewpoint.
The path now descends gently past a clump of trees and swings right. Because of
erosion control, any diversions should be followed. The footpath emerges into Lower
Clent by an inn. Take the alleyway on the left, passing behind the houses. Beyond the
last house, go through a gate and head downhill. Ignore a left fork and, when the main

30

path goes left, turn right to a gateway. Turn left on to the lane to **Clent**. Go over the crossroads by St Leonard's Church into Walton Pool Lane. After $^1/_4$ mile, go through a gate and diagionally across a field to a kissing gate. Go up the drive ahead and climb the stile to the right of a gate. Two more stiles lead into a lane.

The shorter route goes left, here, up Walton Rise and past houses. Now follow a vehicle track on to Walton Hill. There are many side paths here, but keep to the main path as it bears right to rejoin the longer walk.

From the lane, the longer route crosses a stile and the field beyond to a gate. Cross the next field to a stile on to a lane. Turn left to reach (after 1 mile) Calcot Hill Farm. Just before the buildings, climb the stile on the left and follow the well waymarked path along a fence. Go over a stile to join the North Worcestershire Path. Climb a stile past a seat, and keep to the top of the slope, going over two stiles and past another seat. Two more stiles lead past a building: turn left along a track and immediately go right through gorse to the 1033 foot (315m) summit of Walton Hill, where the shorter route is rejoined.

Continue along the ridge, until an arrow points sharp right: from here the path zig-zags downhill, passing a wooden shelter. Where a path crosses a track, turn right down steps to a road. Cross and climb the stile opposite into a field. Aim for the stile in the top left corner, go over and turn left along the lane beyond. At the first turning, go left to reach **St Kenelm's Church**. Continue up the lane past the church to reach a junction. Turn right: the car park is up the hill on the left.

POINTS OF INTEREST:
Clent Hills Country Park – The hills are ideal walking country offering superb views. The Park covers 425 acres of wooded hills, gorse and heather: in early summer the woods are full of bluebells and foxgloves. Animals to be seen include Badgers, Foxes and Fallow Deer from the park at Hagley Hall. Bird life is prolific with, amongst others, Siskins, Redpolls, Yellowhammers and Redstarts. The Four Stones on Adam's Hill are not prehistoric, but were placed here in the 18th century by Lord Lyttleton of nearby Hagley Hall.
Clent – A quaint, peaceful village. St Leonard's Church was largely rebuilt in the 1900s, although the tower dates from the 15th century.
St Kenelm's Church – Dedicated to the boy King of Mercia, murdered in 973 by his sister.

REFRESHMENTS:
The Hill Tavern, Lower Clent.
There is a kiosk at the Visitor Centre and numerous picnic areas.

Walk 17   **EARLSWOOD LAKES**   4m (6$\frac{1}{2}$km)
Maps: OS Sheets Landranger 139; Pathfinder 954.
Beautiful woodlands and lakes which are a haven for wildlife.
Paths can be muddy.
Start: At 116739, the car park off the B4102, Earlswood.

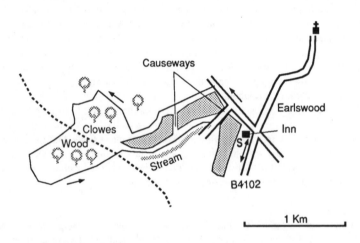

Turn left out of the car park, passing the inn, and turn left again at the crossroads to reach a causeway across **Earlswood Lakes**. Continue across the barrier to the far side of the pool and turn left through a kissing gate by the edge of the lake. After wet weather the path around the pools can be very slippery and eroded in places making it extremely unpleasant underfoot. Go past another causeway in the centre of the lakes and, on reaching two footbridges at the end of the lake, turn right over a footbridge into **Clowes Wood**. Now follow the white arrows, keeping right where the path forks. Walk along the edge of the wood. Just before a timber building, the arrows change to yellow: turn left and follow the main path towards a car park on the edge of Clowes Wood.

Before reaching the car park, turn left along the main path, crossing a footbridge and again following the yellow arrows. Ignore a left turn, and walk straight ahead to reach the edge of the wood. Turn left inside the boundary, go over another footbridge and almost immediately turn right over a railway bridge. On the far side, re-enter the wood on a concessionary path. Keep to the main path and at the top edge of the wood go over a stile by a Nature Reserve sign. Turn left and walk along the edge of the wood. Go over a footbridge and three stiles, and then turn left, still keeping the wood on the left, to go over another stile and footbridge. Two more stiles lead to another footbridge and then the path crosses to the right-hand side of the field, going along a hedge to reach another stile. Turn left and climb a railway bank by another arrow.

Cross the railway line, with care, and descend the steep gravelly path on the other side. Turn right over a stile and follow the path beyond over three stiles in quick succession by another footbridge. Turn right, over the footbridge, and walk between a brook, on the right, and wetland, on the left, to shortly emerge by a lake. Go past a causeway and continue, with the lake on the left, to reach a minor road near the barrier passed earlier. Turn left, and then right by the barrier to reach the crossroads and the car park.

POINTS OF INTEREST:
Earlswood Lakes – The three reservoirs that make up the Lakes were built in 1810 to supply water to the Stratford-upon-Avon canal. They were formed by the damming of two brooks and are a valuable habitat for bird life including Heron, Great Crested Grebes, Moorhens, Coot, Mallard and Canada Geese. The lakes are also very popular with fishermen, and there is a flourishing sailing club.

Earlswood itself is a scattered village which has a timber framed moat house owned by the National Trust. This dates from 1480, but is not open to the public. St Patrick's Church, built in 1840 is almost a mile from the village.
Clowes Wood – The wood, together with New Falling Coppice, is an SSSI. Its 76 acres have been owned and managed by the Warwickshire Wildlife Trust since 1974. Trees include Oak, Birch, Beech, Alder and Rowan. There is also a small area of heathland and a 200 year old hay meadow. The open canopy allows Bluebells, Wood Anemone, Wood Sage and Foxgloves to flourish and the colours in autumn are breathtaking. Please keep to the footpaths to avoid trampling plants.

REFRESHMENTS:
The Reservoir Inn, Earlswood.

Walk 18   **LEEK WOOTTON**   4m (6$\frac{1}{2}$km)

Maps: OS Sheets Landranger 151; Pathfinder 976.

A pleasant ramble around golf courses and farmland. Well waymarked.

Start: At 289688, Leek Wootton Church.

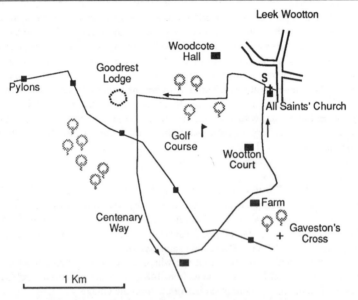

Park with consideration in **Leek Wootton**, where roadside parking is limited, then walk up the lane past the church on to an enclosed path between hedges. Ignore a path to the right, and go over a stile. Walk along the hedge on your left to reach another stile. Here the footpath has been diverted from its original line across the golf course and now turns left, and almost immediately right, to follow the yellow/green marker posts into a spinney. The new path is well waymarked through sections of woodland to a stile on the far side of the course. The earthworks of Goodrest Lodge can be seen in the field to the right. Cross the stile and turn left, following the Centenary Way (*see* Note to Walk 34), with a hedge on your left, across fields. Go over a stile and under pylons, then walk along the edge of a wood, which is also the perimeter of a rifle range.

Emerge from the wood by a sandstone outcrop and follow a diverted path along the right edge of a golf course, walking parallel to a line of pylons. Where the pylons turn left, keep ahead to reach an arrow on the right. Walk along the right edge of a field, following the line indicated by the abundant marker posts, then swing left to reach a stile in the top corner. Go over and keep ahead across the field beyond. On passing a mound, and just before a house, watch for a path on the left. Do not follow the clear Centenary Way path ahead: instead, turn left, cross a stile and turn right along an enclosed path behind houses. Emerge by another house and take the path ahead, to the right of a hedge. Cross the centre of a field, go over a stile and cross another field to a second gateway. Walk under pylons and climb along the left edge of a field, passing a trig. point. The wood on the far right, across fields, houses **Gaveston's Cross**, but this is not accessible.

Descend past farm buildings and follow a path diversion left, and then right, to join a tarmac lane on the golf course. Follow the, by now familiar, yellow/green posts along the lane, swinging left and climbing past Wootton Court to reach a T-junction. Cross straight over and head for a stile in the fence ahead. Another stile and handgate follow in quick succession. Now walk ahead to a gate. Opposite are steps leading into the churchyard of All Saints and the start.

POINTS OF INTEREST:
Leek Wootton – All Saints' Church dates from the 18th century, replacing an earlier building pulled down in 1789. Woodcote Hall, designed by John Gibson in 1861, was a convalescent home during the war, becoming the headquarters of Warwickshire Police in 1949. Goodrest Lodge, demolished in the 19th century, was built by Thomas de Beauchamp and used as a 'rest-house' for the wives of the Earls of Warwick.
Gaveston's Cross – The Cross, on Blacklow Hill, commemorates the execution site of Piers Gaveston, the son of a Gascon knight. Piers was a favourite of Edward II who made him the Earl of Cornwall and Governor of Ireland. The monument was erected in 1821 by Bertie Greatheed, but is on private land. The inscription, composed by Dr Samuel Parr, Rector of Hatton, reads 'In the hollow of this rock, was beheaded on the 1st Day of July 1312, by Barons as lawless as himself, Piers Gaveston, Earl of Cornwall, the Minion of a Hateful King: In Life and Death a memorable instance of misrule'. It is claimed that due to the change in the calendars, the date is incorrect and should read 19th June.

REFRESHMENTS:
The Anchor Inn, Leek Wootton.

Walk 19   **BERKSWELL**   4m (6$\frac{1}{2}$km)

Maps: OS Sheets Landranger 139; Pathfinder 935 and 955.

Delightful walking across parkland and fields. Allow time to explore the fascinating village.

Start: At 245792, the car park by the crossroads, Berkswell.

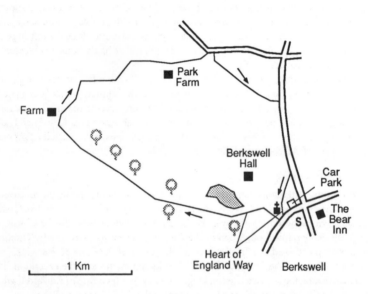

From the car park, turn right past the village green to **Berkswell** Church. Note the stocks (with five holes!) on the green and the well by the church gates, restored in 1851. In the churchyard there is an unusual sandstone War Memorial. Walk past the church, with the wall of the Well House on your left, and go through a gate to join the **Heart of England Way** (*see* Note to Walk 66). Go through a kissing gate, walk ahead and go over a stile on to a raised causeway beside a stream. Go through the trees ahead and turn right, through a kissing gate. Go over a track, leaving the Heart of England Way to join a footpath, with the lake on the right. Please abide by the warning notices and keep to the well-defined footpath across the field. Good views can be enjoyed across the lake to **Berkswell Hall**.

Go over a stile in the top left corner of the field and through a belt of trees. The route is well-trodden as it follows a hedge on the right across two fields. The path then turns inside and along the edge of a pine wood, bordered by spring flowers in season, and passes a pond to reach a stile at the far end of the wood. Follow the hedge on the left, but before reaching the farm buildings, turn right at a fingerpost and walk along the remains of an old hedgerow to reach a stile in a wooden fence. Cross to another stile and the footbridge beyond, then climb up a field and over another stile and footbridge. Follow the fence to your left to reach a tarmac lane. Turn right and follow the lane past Park Farm.

At the junction with a road, go through a gate on the right (beware the finger trapping chain!). Cross the centre of the field beyond to a stile. Go over and follow a well-defined path diagonally across a field to its top left corner. Cross a stile by a gate and walk ahead to reach a stile to the right of a drinking trough. Now ignore the gates and keep the fence on your right to the end of the field. Go through the gate between houses and turn right along a road. Shortly after the village sign, watch for a kissing gate on the right. Go through to rejoin the Heart of England Way. Go over a stile on to the parkland of Berkswell Hall and turn left to a stile in the top left corner. A kissing gate beyond leads into the churchyard.

POINTS OF INTEREST:

Berkswell – The 12th-century St John the Baptist Church has a fine 16th-century oak porch, above which a half-timbered vestry contains the original lead lighted windows and fastenings. The nave dates from 1150 and the chancel has Norman lancet windows at the east end. The superb crypt replaces a much older Saxon crypt: part of the original walls were revealed during restorations in 1968. The pulpit, font and sanctuary chairs are the work of Robert Thompson – look for his 'signature' of carved mice in the woodwork. The churchyard has two unusual graves: a broken pillar on the grave of James Owen signifies his beheading in a sawmill accident in 1898, while James Weetman died of a broken heart in 1840. Another gravestone has carved bread, eggs and bacon, a memorial to a victim of overeating! The Village Museum, run by volunteers, is worth a visit. Outside the inn is a wooden drinking pump with a stone trough and a Russian cannon, captured in 1858 during the Crimean War.

Berkswell Hall – Owned at different times by the Earls of Warwick and Leicester before reverting to the Crown. Since the late 19th century it has belonged to the Wheatley family and is not open to the public.

REFRESHMENTS:
The Bear Inn, Berkswell.

Walk 20   **SOLIHULL**   4m (6½km)

Maps: OS Sheets Landranger 139; Pathfinder 954.

A pleasant circuit across parkland and fields. There is noise from the M42 in the early stages.

Start: At 164792, Brueton Park car park.

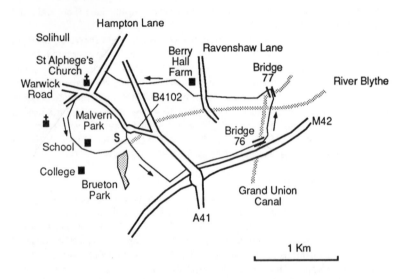

The car park can be reached from the B4102 roundabout, just off the A41.

Turn right from the car park down the old Warwick Road, passing the lake and crossing Sandalls Bridge over the River Blythe. At the end of the road, turn left into Barston Lane. For the next mile the noise of the M42 can be intrusive. At the end of the road, take the tarmac path ahead and cross the A41 with care. The path continues to the right of the lamppost opposite, not down either of the tarmac lanes on the left. Go through a gate then walk between fences, parallel to the motorway. Go through another gate to reach a tarmac footpath and follow it Bridge 76 at Henwood Wharf. Turn left up the towpath of the Grand Union Canal (*see* Note to Walk 5).

Continue to the next bridge (No. 77), turning left over the bridge and immediately going left through a gateway. Go down the track beyond, between fences, to reach a

38

stile in the corner, passing a sign erected by a friendly landowner warning all trespassers they will be shot! Go over the stile and follow the hedge on the right across the next three fields, linked by stiles, to reach a gate on to Ravenshaw Lane. Cross, go over the stile opposite and keep the fence on your right to go through a gate in the field's top right corner into a wood. Walk between the wood and the fence behind Berry Hall farm (beware of the dogs in the fenced compound). Go over a stile and follow the hedge on the left along a partly gravelled path, passing a metal gateway and going over another stile. Continue through a small area of woodland, with a ruined building on the left, to reach a stile. Walk across two fields, with the hedge on your right, aiming for the top right corner to reach two kissing gates. Go through to reach the **Solihull** by-pass.

Cross, with care, and go between houses to reach Marsh Lane. Walk up Oakley Wood Drive opposite, and at the end, by No. 19, continue up a path to Hampton Lane. Turn left to the traffic lights on Warwick Road. Cross over, turn right, and almost immediately left into New Road. Turn left into Malvern Park and follow the main path past a play area, an impressive horse statue and tennis courts. Go between a school and a college into Brueton Park. At the end of the park the path splits, the left branch going through a wildlife compound and the right branch skirting its edge. Both paths meet on the far side, from where it is a short step back to the car park.

POINTS OF INTEREST:

Solihull – The town has many features of interest including Malvern Hall, which was built by the Greswolde family in the 18th century and now houses Solihull school. A Constable painting of the Hall hangs in the Tate Gallery. The original forest settlement grew around the first church, which was built about 1220. The town was granted a charter for a market in 1242. St Alphege's Church dates from 1270 and has a spire 168 feet high, although the steeple was blown down in 1757. The nave was partly rebuilt at the time of the Black Death, with the walls and pillars remaining open to the sky for many years. The north chapel window depicts the murder of Thomas à Becket. A fine bronze statue of a horse by Boehms, given in 1875 by Captain Bird in memory of his father, can be found in Malvern Park. The 13th-century Sandalls Bridge was named after John de Sandale who was Chancellor of England under Edward II.

REFRESHMENTS:

There is plenty of choice in Solihull.

Walk 21   **DUNCHURCH AND DRAYCOTE WATER**   4m (6½km)
Maps: OS Sheets Landranger 140; Pathfinder 956.
*Easy ramble from attractive village, skirting a reservoir which
is marvellous for birds.*
Start: At 486713, the crossroads in the centre of Dunchurch.

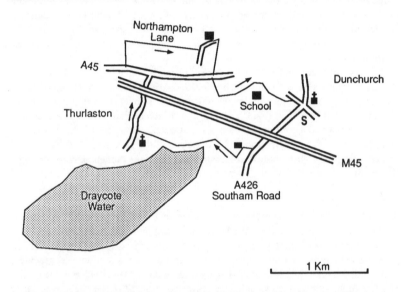

Parking is limited to Dunchurch's side streets as the centre can be very congested.

From the crossroads, walk down the Southam road (the A426) and go over the M45. Turn down the first lane on the right, by a post box. Just before the first house, turn left along a path, following it to a driveway. Go right, beside the fence and over the stile opposite into a field. Head downhill across the field and go through a gate on to a track. Turn left to reach two gates and go over a stile on the right. Now keep the fence on your left to reach a stile in the left corner from where there are fine views over **Draycote Water**. This bay, particularly in winter when the reservoir is quieter, is excellent for bird-watching. Draycote Water is home to significant numbers of wildfowl and the gull roost at sunset is an amazing spectacle. During the spring and autumn bird migrations, Draycote is worth watching for rarities.

40

Follow the path through the wood, go over a stile and walk up a concrete track. Pass through a gate on to a lane in **Thurlaston**. Go past the church and walk ahead to reach a T-junction. Turn right, cross the M45 again and continue to reach the A45. Cross, with care, and turn left along the road, passing a garage to reach a road sign. Now go through a gap in the hedge on the right and follow the hedge on the right to join a broad, muddy track, Northampton Lane, once part of the main route between Coventry and Northampton.

Turn right along this bridleway, following it to join a lane. Turn left and follow the lane round a bend. Shortly after the last house on the left, turn right through a hedge gap and walk straight across the field beyond, passing a power pole, then following a bank on the left to reach the A45. Cross, with care, and go down the lane opposite. At its end, go through the gate on the left and follow the hedge on the left to reach a stile in the corner. Go over and follow an enclosed path beside a school playing field to reach a road. Turn right, then left past the school and keep on down the road to reach the crossroads in **Dunchurch**.

POINTS OF INTEREST:

Draycote Water – At more than 600,000 acres, this is the largest area of open water in Warwickshire. It was completed in 1970 and is used as a storage reservoir. It is filled during the winter with water pumped from the River Leam, which helps to reduce river flooding. The huge expanse of water caters for activities such as sailing, windsurfing, fishing, walking and bird-watching. However, as the reservoir is owned by Severn Trent Water, public access is not automatically allowed and permits are essential for all activities, including walking! (Tel: 01788 811107). The one exception is the Country Park on the south side of the reservoir, which has car parking and picnic sites for all to enjoy. This small area, 21 acres, was established in 1972 and rises to Hensborough Hill which affords excellent views over the reservoir.

Thurlaston – In the 14th century monks built the chapel dedicated to St Edmund and in 1849 the present brick church was constructed.

Dunchurch – The village stands on an old coaching route between London and the Midlands. At the crossroads is an imposing statue of Lord Montague Douglas Scott erected by his tenants in 1867. The Almshouses were built in 1693 and rebuilt in 1818. St Peter's Church has earlier Norman work in the chancel walls but was mostly built in the 14th century. It was one of the first to be supplied with gas, by a private company in 1872, before even Rugby had its own gas supply.

REFRESHMENTS:
There is plenty of choice in Dunchurch.

Walk 22   **THE WELCOMBE HILLS**   4½m (7km)

Maps: OS Sheets Landranger 151; Pathfinder 997 and 998.

An undulating walk to a marvellous viewpoint in the Country Park overlooking Stratford. Paths can be muddy.

Start: At 207548, the Tourist Information Centre, Bridgefoot.

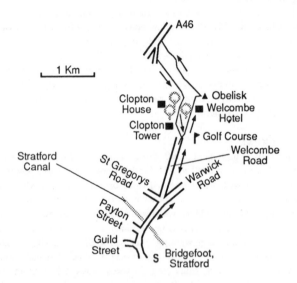

Turn right, crossing the busy Warwick road, with care, at the traffic lights. Go over Guild Street, passing a garage. After crossing Payton Street and the canal bridge, take the next left turning, up St Gregorys road, going almost immediately right into Welcombe road. At the top, go through a handgate, on the right, into the open grassland of the **Welcombe Hills**. Follow the well-defined path which climbs beside a hedge on the right. Go through a kissing gate, and walk past a golf course, on the right. As you climb, the **Obelisk** comes into view ahead.

After going through another kissing gate, ignore a left fork in the path and keep the hedge on your right to go through another gate and past the Welcombe Hotel. The path now climbs steadily and care is needed as it can be slippery when muddy. Maintain direction, but immediately after the end of the wall, turn right and go over a stile.

42

Climb to the Obelisk and enjoy the views, stretching from Edge Hill to the Cotswolds. Now retrace your steps towards the stile, but just before it, turn right, and then left through a metal gate. Walk straight up the enclosed lane beyond and go through a gateway. The lane continues for almost a mile, with good views across to Snitterfield, on the right, to reach the A46. Turn left, with care, and after about 50 yards go left down a minor road passing several houses and then taking a path, on the left, which runs by a hedgerow and a wire fence on the right.

Go through a gate, ignoring a stile on the right, and walk alongside a field to enter a small area of woodland. The path splits in two to avoid the worst of the mud, but the paths meet at a gate on the far side of the wood. Go through and turn right. The path beyond descends gradually, first across open grassland, then into woods and past a covered reservoir into a lane. Continue down the lane to Clopton Tower. **Clopton House** is further down the lane, on the right. Go over a stile to the left of Clopton Tower and head diagonally left across the field beyond to rejoin the outward route in the top corner. Retrace the outward route back to the start.

POINTS OF INTEREST:
The Welcombe Hills – The Hills were left to the people of Stratford by Flowers, the brewing family. They cover 70 acres, with woods and grassland, and offer wonderful walking, with extensive views over the Warwickshire plain. These hills were the scene of a brief skirmish during the Civil War, in January 1643, between Colonel Wagstaffe, who commanded a troop of Royalist horse, and Lord Brooke, who led a parliamentary force out of Warwick.
Obelisk – This striking landmark is 120 feet high and made of Welsh granite. It was erected in 1876 to commemorate the Philips family, successful cotton manufacturers in the mid-1800s, who were responsible for building the mansion, now the Welcombe Hotel, passed on the walk.
Clopton House – The House dates from the 16th century, but was much enlarged in the 17th by Sir John Clopton, and remodelled again in the 18th. Its most famous occupant was Sir Hugh Clopton, who restored the Guild Chapel in Stratford. He was also a Lord Mayor of London during the reign of Henry VII. The house, which is private, is supposedly haunted by the ghost of Charlotte Clopton who was entombed prematurely during the plague of 1564. Perhaps that is where the idea for the ending of *Romeo and Juliet* came from!

REFRESHMENTS:
There is a wide choice in Stratford-upon-Avon and a picnic area at the obelisk.

Walks 23 & 24 **HARTSHILL AND THE COVENTRY CANAL** $4^1/_2$m (7km)
or 6m ($9^1/_2$km)

Maps: OS Sheets Landranger 140; Pathfinder 914.
Golf courses, farm lanes, a towpath and delightful woodland.
Start: At 316944, Hartshill Hayes Country Park car park.

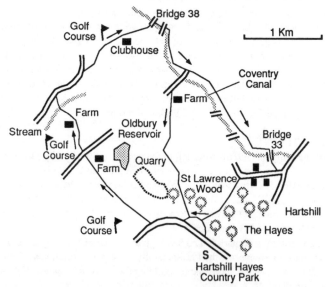

Go past a marker post (No. 1), on to open hillside passing a covered reservoir on the left. Follow the railings, left, through a gate and turn right along a lane through Oldbury. After $^1/_4$ mile, before a farm drive on the left, turn right along a well-marked bridleway across a golf course. Follow the white posts, leaving the course by the corner of the last green. Maintain direction across a field, staying by a fence, and then a hedge, on the right, to reach a road to the left of farm buildings. Cross and go down the drive opposite, passing through the farmyard and going straight on through a metal gate. Drop downhill, with a brook on the left, go over a stile, and along a path. Cross another brook and climb across another golf course to reach a road. Turn right and after $^1/_4$ mile, right again down a drive to Outwoods Farm, by green boxes. Go past the farmhouse and through a metal gate on to yet another golf course. Follow the bridleway

44

signs along the right-hand boundary, passing the clubhouse to join a muddy lane. This leads to a bridge (No. 38) over the **Coventry Canal**. Follow the towpath, with the canal on your right, to reach a second bridge (No. 36).

The shorter route goes right here, crossing the bridge and going up the road. When the road swings right, go left, up a lane past farm buildings and through the gate ahead. Now climb a slope along a bridleway, go through a gateway and turn right, following a hedge. Go through another gateway and drop downhill, turning left at the bottom, past a metal gate on to an enclosed path. The well-signed bridleway now follows field edges to reach a corner of St Lawrence Wood. Here, the main path (with numbered posts) leads uphill, through the wood, passing The Hayes to reach the start.

The longer route continues along the towpath to bridge No. 33. There, turn right and cross a field to reach a gap in the hedge. Turn right along the lane on the outskirts of **Hartshill Green**, passing houses and Cherry Tree Farm. When the lane descends and swings right, go through the first metal gate on the left and cross half-right to reach the corner of woodland. Go over a stile and keep straight ahead, by the fence on the right, uphill, at the edge of the wood. The wood on the left is part of **Hartshill Hayes Country Park** and is well worth exploring. Go past an adventure playground, up steps and turn left to reach the start.

POINTS OF INTEREST:

Coventry Canal – Opened in 1790, its completion having taken over 20 years. It runs from Coventry to Fradley and is now a very popular holiday route.

Hartshill Green – The village has a memorial bus shelter, built in 1972, as a monument to the 17th-century poet Michael Drayton who was born here. Hartshill Castle was an 11th-century motte and bailey castle and one of its Lords, Robert de Hartshill, was killed alongside Simon de Montfort at the Battle of Evesham in 1265.

Hartshill Hayes Country Park – The 136 acres here were made a Country Park in 1978. The open hilltop has views stretching across the Anker valley into Leicestershire, towards Charnwood Forest. St Lawrence Wood commemorates a 10th-century chapel. The Hayes has a group of oaks planted around 120 years ago. Nearby, on private land, is a Roman hill fort. The grassland flowers attract a variety of insects and the woods are home to birds such as Coal Tit, Chiffchaff, Spotted Flycatcher, Chaffinch, Sparrowhawk, Woodcock, Jay and Wren. Alder grows in the wetter parts and in many places Hazel, Elder and Holly thrive.

REFRESHMENTS:

The Stag and Pheasant, Hartshill Green.

There is also a kiosk at the Country Park Visitor Centre.

Walk 25   SANDWELL VALLEY PARK   4¹/₂m (7km)

Maps: OS Sheets Landranger 139; Pathfinder 913.

A surprising oasis in the middle of an urban area, with plenty of natural history interest.

Start: At 029913, a car park, Forge Lane.

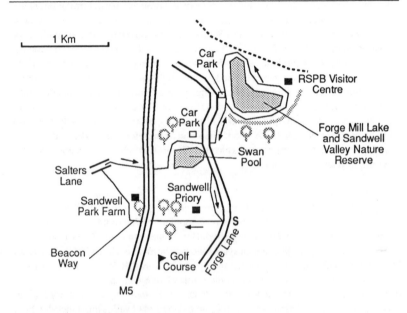

Car parks around **Sandwell Valley Country Park** are numerous and it is possible to begin the walk from any of those mentioned.

From the rear of the car park at Forge Lane, go straight ahead along a gravel path. Go between woodland and a golf course, past the remains of Sandwell Priory, and cross a bridge over the M5. Turn right, down steps, to go along the Beacon Way (*see* Note to Walk 95). Where the path forks, branch left and go over three footbridges to reach **Sandwell Park Farm**. With your back to the main entrance, head north-west across grass, aiming to the left of a tower block on the horizon. Just before a car park, turn right over a footbridge, go through a handgate and climb a field, parallel to the road. Turn right at the top, past Warstone House, and go through a gate into Salters

Lane. This path leads down through fields with marvellous views. Ignore side paths and cross the motorway again, over another footbridge. Turn left, still on the Beacon Way, and pass Swan Pool, on the right.

Go through another car park, then cross a road to a Beacon Way signpost. Follow this, left, across grassland to reach Forge Mill Lake car park. Go right, over a footbridge, and turn right between Forge Mill Lake and a stream, soon reaching Sandwell Valley Nature Reserve. Dogs should be on a lead and under strict control to minimise disturbance to bird life. As with all Nature Reserves, only the quiet walker will be rewarded with good views of wildlife. Paths to the left lead to the bird hides, but the main path climbs to the **RSPB Visitor Centre**. Go past the Centre and take a path to the left, past another hide, and shortly swing left, downhill, to go over a footbridge on to the lakeside. This path collects all the water running off nearby fields and can be very squelchy. Go straight over at a crosstracks to reach the end of the lake by the railway. Turn left and walk along the raised bank, still with the lake on the left, back to Forge Mill car park. Reverse the outward path to Swan Pool car park, and turn left by the lake. Leave the shore at the first corner, going left along a grassy path. Now continue parallel with a hedge across open grassland, cross another track and walk between hedges to return to the start.

POINTS OF INTEREST:

Sandwell Valley Country Park – Once a coal mine on the Earl of Dartmouth's estate, when the mine closed the land was given to local people and developed into 2,000 acres of parkland. A series of artificial lakes were constructed to hold floodwaters, thereby benefiting the wildfowl, and the spoil from the site was used to landscape the area. Sandwell Priory is all that remains of a 12th-century Benedictine monastery closed in 1525 on the orders of Cardinal Wolsey. Sandwell Hall, built on the site of the priory in 1705, was demolished in 1928.

Sandwell Park Farm – The farm was originally built in 1705 as part of the Earl of Dartmouth's estate. Restored in 1981, it is now a farm showing traditional Victorian farming practices. Craft workshops and sheep shearing demonstrations can be seen, as well as farm breeds appropriate to the period. There is also a Heritage Centre housing finds from the 1980s archaeological dig at Sandwell Priory.

RSPB Visitor Centre – The RSPB's Reserve is home to Tufted Duck, Coot, Moorhen, Little Ringed Plover, Lapwing, Snipe, Whitethroat, Reed, Sedge and Willow Warblers. A mud scrape also attract waders. In total, over 130 species have been recorded.

REFRESHMENTS:
There are tea rooms at Sandwell Park Farm.

CLIFFORD CHAMBERS $4^1/_2$m (7km)
or $9^1/_2$m (15km)

Maps: OS Sheets Landranger 151; Pathfinder 997, 998 and 1021.
An invigorating walk along a disused railway, with a longer option to interesting villages.
Start: At 196541, Seven Meadows Road car park, Stratford.

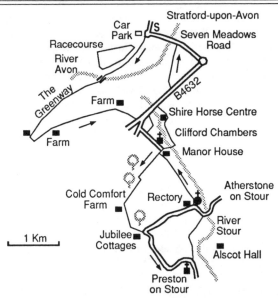

Walk westwards, following **The Greenway** for almost 2 miles. At the first house, turn left along a lane, passing two farms to reach the B4632. Turn left, with care, to reach a stile on the right, before a bridge.

The shorter walk continues along the B4362, rejoining the longer walk at a farm track on the right.

The longer route crosses the stile and goes along the left edge of a field. Go through a kissing gate and alongside the River Stour. Go through another kissing gate, along the left edge of a lawn and up a lane. Turn left through **Clifford Chambers**, passing the church to reach the end of the main street, by the manor house. Go right through a gate and, where the lane turns left, walk uphill, beside a hedge, towards a wood. Go left by the

48

wood, then right to a gate. Go along a hedge, switching sides halfway. Go downhill towards Cold Comfort Farm, turning left at the bottom to reach the field's end. Now aim for a stile by a plantation. Turn left up the lane, passing Jubilee Cottages and turning right along a road into **Preston on Stour**. From the front of the churchyard, cross the green and turn left up the middle lane by a timber cottage. Go through a kissing gate into Alscot Park. Pass a grassy mound, on the left, go through a gate and turn right beside a plantation. At its end, turn right on to a path to Atherstone on Stour. Turn left, past an old church (now a private house) and at a left bend, by a Georgian rectory, take the path ahead. Cross two fields to a small building where a path leads to Clifford Chambers. Turn right, past the manor house, go through a gate to the left of a drive and cross the river. Go through a gate and follow a fence past old fish ponds, on the right. Turn left over a bridge and go left across a field. Go through a kissing gate, across the centre of the next field and over a stile. Now head for a gate halfway along the fence on the right. Go over a stile and walk to the right of farm buildings to reach a T-junction. Turn left along a farm track past the **Shire Horse Centre** to reach the B4632. Turn right, rejoining the shorter route.

Go along the road, then climb a stile on the left and follow the left edge of the field beyond. Go through a gate on to a tarmac path, dropping downhill to a stile. Turn left, then right by the river and cross the pedestrian bridge. Turn left, back under the road bridge, and then turn right to the car park.

POINTS OF INTEREST:

The Greenway – Once a railway and now a footpath and cycleway from Stratford to Long Marston.

Clifford Chambers – The manor house was held by the Rainsford family in the 16th century. It was gutted by fire and rebuilt by Sir Edwin Lutyens following the First World War. The Norman church of St Helen was restored in 1886 and contains tombs of the Rainsford family.

Preston on Stour – St Mary the Virgin's Church was rebuilt by James West in the 1750s and has a 15th-century tower and nave. A stained glass window has several royal crests and arms, including the crown within a hawthorn bush adopted by Henry VII after Bosworth Field. Alscot Park was built on the site of an old monastery and a deserted village and was bought by James West in 1749.

Shire Horse Centre – Open all year with wagon and pony rides, a nature trail and rare farm breeds.

REFRESHMENTS:

The New Inn, Clifford Chambers.

There is a restaurant at the Shire Horse Centre.

Walk 28 THE LEASOWES AND HALESOWEN ABBEY $4^{1}/_{2}$m (7km)

Maps: OS Sheets Landranger 139; Pathfinder 933.

A walk across marvellous countryside near Halesowen. Good paths with excellent waymarking.

Start: At 975843, Leasowes car park.

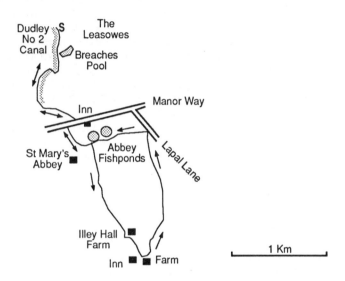

Before starting the walk, do not miss exploring the numerous woodland and stream-side paths through the delightful **Leasowes** park.

Take the path, at the rear of the car park, going along the towpath of the now derelict Dudley No. 2 canal. Pass Breaches Pool, below on the left, to reach the junction of four paths. Keep right, along the towpath, crossing a footbridge over the canal. Continue to the end of the canal, passing the filled-in end to reach a tarmac path. Turn left, then right past a playground. Cross the very busy Manor Way with care, and turn right, and shortly left, over a stile. Walk with a hedge on your left and go over another stile. The ruins of **St Mary's Abbey** are ahead. Go half-left to cross a footbridge, turn left through the remains of the Abbey fishponds and cross a stile on the right.

Follow the fence on the right to reach a stile. Go over to join a farm track, turning left and swinging right over a stream. Turn left, with a hedge on your right, passing a footbridge, on the left, to reach the top corner of a field. Climb a hidden stile by the gate and turn left along the edge of two fields, with a stream to the left, to reach the drive of Illey Hall Farm. Turn left, then right, before the farm, to reach a football field. Do not cross the field: instead, turn left to the corner, cross the right-hand stile and turn right up the field edge. Cross two stiles in quick succession to reach another drive. The inn lies to the right here. Turn left and, at the end of the drive, swing left over a stile and a stream. The path curves right, past a hedge and across a field (ignore a path on the left) to another stile. Cross to the stile ahead and keep the wood on your left to reach a stile halfway along. Turn left, through the wood, to cross a stream and walk between hedges. Pass between 4 posts (ignore a stile on the left) and continue until the lane swings right. Now go left between wooden posts and along an enclosed path (ignoring any stiles on the left), going between more posts. Turn left over a stile and then right down the hill to Lapal Lane. Do not cross the stile; instead, turn left, with a hedge on your right, through two fields. In the third field, turn right and, shortly, go over a stile and turn left alongside the hedge. Soon you rejoin the outward path: retrace your steps back to the start.

POINTS OF INTEREST:

Leasowes Park – This ancient woodland was landscaped by William Shenstone after he inherited it in 1742. After Shenstone's death, in 1763, The Leasowes passed through many hands: Dudley Council now plans to restore it to its former glory. The Council publish excellent, informative leaflets covering The Leasowes and the countryside around the Abbey.

St Mary's Abbey – The Manor of Hales, which once covered 10,000 acres, was granted by William the Conqueror to Roger de Montgomery, Earl of Shrewsbury, and then to David-ap-Owen in 1177. It reverted to King John who later donated the land to the Bishop of Winchester. The Abbey was founded in 1215 by the White Canons, but partly demolished at the Dissolution and given to Sir John Dudley. It was bought by John Lyttleton in 1560. The present owner is Viscount Cobham. The cloister is now part of Manor Abbey Farm. The rest of the stone was used to build nearby Hagley Hall. Access is limited to the Abbey Infirmary on the few open days.

REFRESHMENTS:
The Black Horse, Manor Way, Halesowen.
The Black Horse, Illey.

Walk 29   **CORLEY** $4^1/_2$m (7km)

Maps: OS Sheets Landranger 140; Pathfinder 935.

A pleasant easy ramble passing the site of a hill fort. Some road walking. Well waymarked.

Start: At 304844, a lay-by on the B4098 south of Corley.

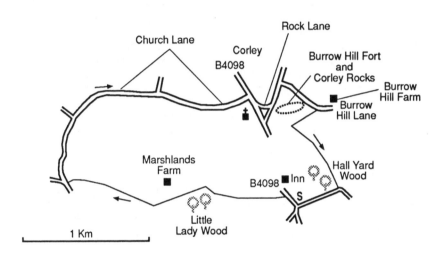

The lay-by is not an official parking spot so please show consideration to residents. There is also limited parking in Church Lane and, possibly, by Burrow Hill but the smashed windscreen glass lying around indicates this may not be very safe!

From the lay-by, take the footpath on the right by the county boundary sign. Go through a gate and over a stile. Head for a stile in the top left corner of the field ahead. Go over and keep the mature holly hedges on your left across two fields. (The third field and the fields beyond are part of horse gallops, some fields having loose horses, so please keep dogs on a lead.) Climb up the field, with the hedge on your left, to a stile that is part of a jump. Cross to a wood. Keep the edge of Little Lady Wood on

your left across two fields and, when the wood ends, keep the hedge on your left, ignoring a stile, also on the left, to reach a double stile, with Marshlands Farm away to the right. Follow a hedge across three fields to reach a minor road.

Turn right to a T-junction. Go right along Church Lane for a mile into **Corley**. At the junction near the church, turn right along the B4098 and, shortly, left down Rock Lane. Turn left at a junction, going through Corley Rocks and then turning right along Burrow Hill Lane. Look for the exposed sandstone rocks on the right – the hillfort once occupied the top of the hill. Where the lane bends left by Burrow Hill Farm, turn right over a stile and climb the enclosed lane beyond.

At the top, in the field on the right, the other side of the hillfort, with the remains of the earthen ramparts, can be seen. Where the hedge ends, turn left, along the hedge, towards Hall Yard Wood. Just before the wood, go over a stile on the left and turn right to skirt the wood edge. Go over a stile and follow the edge of pasture to reach a lane. Turn right up the hill to reach the B4098: the starting lay-by lies to the right.

POINTS OF INTEREST:
Corley – The village is situated on a sandstone ridge nearly 600 feet above sea level and offers extensive views to the north. The exposed red sandstone known as Corley Rocks forms part of the Iron Age hill fort passed on the walk. The parish church has a font inscribed 1661 and a Norman nave. The village war memorial is in the lychgate.

REFRESHMENTS:
The Horse and Jockey, Corley.

Walk 30   **HAMPTON IN ARDEN AND BARSTON** $4\frac{1}{2}$m (7km)
Maps: OS Sheets Landranger 139; Pathfinder 935 and 955.
A pleasant walk by the River Blythe and a lake, returning across fields. Well waymarked.
Start: At 213803, Marsh Lane car park, Hampton.

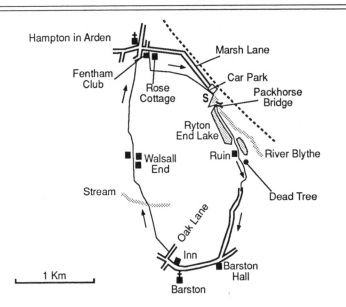

At the far end of the car park, turn right along the signed bridleway. Keep the pond on your left to reach the lake at Ryton End. This was once a quarry and is now an excellent habitat for wildfowl. Turn left around the shoreline, passing the 500 year old packhorse bridge on the left, to the end of the lake. Now keep straight on, past a ruined building on the right, to reach a junction of paths, with a footbridge on the left. Walk ahead, past a pond and a dead tree on the left, to join a dirt track. Turn left, alongside the river, and follow a private road which merges with a minor road at a gateway. Go along the road to a T-junction. Turn right into Barston (*see* Note to Walk 93).

Go past Barston Hall, the church and the inn, then turn right into Oak Lane. A short distance along on the left, take the footpath between houses Nos. 20 and 22. Go over a stile into a field and follow the hedge on the left to another stile. Cross and

follow the hedge on the right to yet another stile. Cross the centre of the next two fields to reach a stile and a bridge over a stream. Cross, aim uphill towards the cluster of houses at Walsall End and go over the stile in the top left corner of the field. Turn left along a lane, passing cottages to reach a cattle grid. Beyond this, turn immediately right over another cattle grid, walk past Oak Tree Cottage and cross the stile on the right. Follow the hedge on the left, and where it ends, continue to the field end. Go over a bridge and straight across a lane to a stile. Follow the hedge on the right over a long field to reach a stile in the top right corner. Aim for the top right corner of the next field, cross two stiles in quick succession and head for the top right corner of the field beyond. The enclosed path beyond leads to a lane: turn right into **Hampton in Arden**.

Turn right and, at a sharp bend opposite the church, go down Marsh Lane. Just past the Fentham Club, take the path on the right, by Rose Cottage. Go over the stile and walk ahead to cross another stile by a gate. At the end of the next field, by a redundant stile, turn left through the gap. Follow the hedge and fence on the left to a stile on to a lane by houses. Turn left and go up the drive directly ahead. Go over a stile and down the enclosed path into a field. Cross the centre of the next three fields, linked by stiles to reach the start of the bridleway taken earlier. Turn left to return to the car park.

POINTS OF INTEREST:

Hampton in Arden – The village was a Saxon settlement in the 7th century and once stood on the salt way running from Droitwich to Coventry. The manor house was purchased by Sir Robert Peel for his son Frederick, who was responsible for the church alterations in 1879. St Mary and St Bartholomew Church, begun in 1130, has a rare heart shrine in the chancel, where a kneeling figure holds a shield below a trefoiled arch. The spire was struck by lightning in 1643 and never rebuilt. The chief glory is the magnificent east window, with stained glass depicting Shakespeare, Milton, Dryden, Cowper and Shelley – whose niece married Frederick Peel. The mid-19th-century cottages near the church have tile hangings on the walls and unusual plaster patterns.

REFRESHMENTS:
The White Lion, Hampton in Arden.
The Bull's Head, Barston.

Walk 31　　　**COMPTON AND WIGHTWICK**　　　$4^1/_2$m (7km)

Maps: OS Sheets Landranger 139; Pathfinder 912.

A pleasant walk along a canal towpath, past a National Trust manor and returning along a disused railway.

Start: At 883988, Compton.

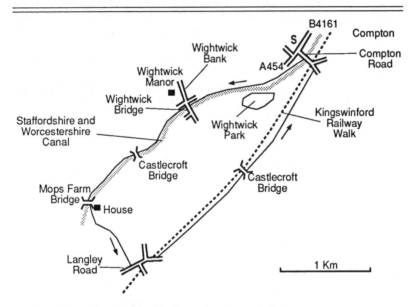

Please park with consideration in Compton as space is limited.

From the junction of the B4161 and the A454, walk down Compton Road towards the **Staffordshire and Worcestershire Canal**. Turn right, westwards along the towpath, following it past Wightwick Family Park and several locks to reach Wightwick Bridge. To reach **Wightwick Manor**, leave the canal here and walk up Wightwick Bank.

Return to the towpath and continue along the canal, going under Castlecroft Bridge and continuing for nearly a mile to reach Mops Farm Bridge. Leave the canal here, turning left over the bridge, then right by houses to reach a gateway. Follow the

hedge on the left to reach a stile by a gate. Go over and cross the field beyond. At the end of the next field, the path switches sides of the hedge: continue along it to reach Langley Road.

Turn left. Now, do not take the lane on the right: instead, take the steps on the right which give access to the **Kingswinford Railway Walk**. Turn left and proceed along the dismantled railway for nearly two miles, going under another Castlecroft Bridge to reach the bridge in Compton. Here a left turn leads back to the start.

POINTS OF INTEREST:

Staffordshire and Worcestershire Canal – The canal was built by James Brindley to link the Midlands with the River Severn and opened in 1722. It runs for 46 miles, from Great Haywood to Stourport, and passes through lovely, unspoilt countryside. The circular side weirs are unique to this canal and occupy less space than a conventional weir of equal capacity. Awbridge Lock is crossed by the only original bridge remaining on the canal, and is believed to be Brindley's first attempt at building a canal bridge and a lock on a public road. The bridge parapet is unusual, having nine brick pillars.

Wightwick Manor – Now in the care of the National Trust, this beautiful half-timbered mansion dates from 1887. Fine examples of William Morris fabrics and wallpapers, glass by Kempe and de Morgan-ware can be seen. The garden has yew hedges and fine topiary, and contains two pools. The Manor is open from March to December on Thursday and Saturday afternoons plus Bank Holidays. The gardens are open Wednesday and Thursday and Bank Holidays. Please telephone before you visit to check the opening times. Tel: 01902 761108.

Kingswinford Railway Walk – This 5$^1/_2$ mile linear walk follows the line of a disused railway. The single track Kingswinford Branch Railway opened in 1925 to connect Wolverhampton with Kingswinford, but services were withdrawn in 1932. Himley station was built for the convenience of the Earl of Dudley and his guests.

REFRESHMENTS:

The Swan, Compton.

There is a Tea Room at Wightwick Manor, open on Wednesdays, Thursdays and Bank Holidays.

Walk 32   **WOLSTON AND BRANDON** $4^1/_2$m (7km)

Maps: OS Sheets Landranger 140; Pathfinder 956.

An easy ramble across fields. Can be muddy and not for anyone afraid of cattle!

Start: At 414755, the B4029 crossroads, Wolston.

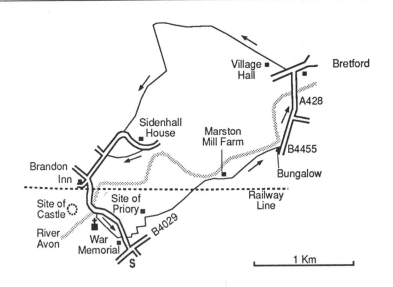

There is limited roadside parking by the B4029 crossroads in **Wolston**.

To start the walk, stand with your back to the newsagents at the T-junction and walk up the road to reach an alleyway on the right opposite the war memorial. Go down the alleyway to Larchfields Road, at the end of which, turn right into Meadow Road. Go left into Priory Lane. Follow the lane as it swings sharp right: in the fields on the left is the site of the old priory. Go under a railway bridge and over a cattle grid on to the drive to Marston Mill Farm. Follow the drive, then turn right in front of the farmhouse and left before the barns. Keep on the dirt track ahead, with a fence on the right, going through fields usually full of cattle – please keep dogs on a lead. When the track swings right, stay ahead through a gateway and cross the next field. At the time of writing there was a bull loose in this field, so keep your eyes peeled! The path

keeps the river on the left, becoming enclosed between the riverbank and trees: continue to reach a stile by a bungalow (beware of the dog!). Go over and turn left along a drive to reach the B4455. An unpleasant stretch of road walking with no pavement follows, so please be careful. At the junction, bear left along the A428, again with care, and cross the River Avon to reach a T-junction in Bretford.

Turn left and immediately cross over to the left-hand tarmac drive, ignoring the bridleway, signed to Brinklow, on the right. Keep straight on, passing the village hall and going along a sunken path, following a barbed wire fence on the right to reach the next field. Turn right, and almost immediately left. Now stay between the hedge and fence wires for a mile, going through a metal gate and past a pond to join another track. Turn left through a copse and, after 100 yards, turn left along another bridleway. Follow this between fences, swing right to go through a wooden gate. Follow the hedge on the right to reach a road.

Turn left, passing Sidenhall House on the left. Now go over a stile on the right and head across the field beyond to reach a stile by a telegraph pole. Go over and aim diagonally right to another stile, by conifers, and a gate on to a drive. Go down the drive to a road and turn left into Brandon. At the next junction, by the inn, turn left under the railway bridge. Beyond the bridge, in the fields on the right, are the earthworks of **Brandon Castle**. Continue along the pavement and over the footbridge across the river. Turn right to reach the church, then turn left beside meadows and go past the school to reach the war memorial near the start.

POINTS OF INTEREST:
Wolston – The oldest part of the village is very attractive with a brook running through the centre, spanned at intervals by tiny bridges. St Margaret's Church is in a lovely setting amid meadows and near old parkland. It has a Norman south doorway. The north transept window has been altered twice, once in 1571 and again in 1624. The walk passes the site of a Benedictine Priory founded in the 11th century. The old Manor House was dismantled earlier this century and taken to America where it was re-assembled stone by stone.

Brandon Castle – Once occupied by the de Verdon family, the castle was destroyed, possibly by Simon de Montfort, around 1266. The site now belongs to riding stables and is used as part of a jumping course.

REFRESHMENTS:
The Queen's Head, Bretford
The Royal Oak, Brandon.
There are several possibilities in Wolston.

Walk 33   KINGSBURY WATER PARK   5m (8km)

Maps: OS Sheets Landranger 139; Pathfinder 914.

A walk round a wildlife haven, with a detour to Kingsbury Church. Some areas can be muddy.

Start: At 204959, the Visitor Centre car park.

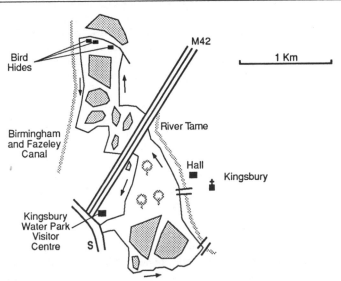

From **Kingsbury Water Park** car park, walk towards the Sailing Club and take the Nature Trail route along a lane. Go through the gate at the far end into mixed woodland. The path follows a raised causeway to reach a lake. Go through a gate on the right and along a path between hedges. Soon, the path runs between a road and a lake, then curves left and moves away from the water's edge, passing farm buildings and going through a gate. Turn right, away, from the Nature Trail, and cross a road. Look for the numbered waymarks as the path follows the edge of another lake, crosses a road, and goes round Causeway Pool (Waymark 6). On reaching a small car park, take the path half-right (Waymark 7) and go past Swann Pool. At a path fork, take the left branch, going over a footbridge and between lakes to reach another minor road. Cross the road on to open grassland. Now keep a hedge on the right and a lake on the left, and aim for the houses ahead.

On reaching the River Tame, turn left and walk, with the river on your right, to a footbridge. Cross this (the raised causeway is evidence that this area can flood in winter), and climb steps to **Kingsbury** Church. Return the same way over the footbridge and turn right, following the riverside path past playing fields and another pool. Cross a stile and a footbridge, and aim for the underpass of the M42 directly ahead. Beyond the underpass, turn left to follow a narrow path between bushes. The path emerges on to a raised bank: turn right and follow the path, first left, and then right over a footbridge. Turn right and go over another footbridge to reach a path fork at the Nature Reserve sign. Take the left branch, keeping to the right-hand side of the lakes. Ignore all left paths until you arrive at a bird hide. Here the path swings to the left, still following the edge of the lake, going past two more hides and then turning left alongside a canal. Just before some houses, the path turns left and winds past two more lakes to emerge at a car park. At the far end of the car park, take the right-hand path, turning right again at a Heart of England Way sign. Walk past fields to reach a T-junction. Turn left and go back under the M42 (a different underpass this time!). Now go past another lake, turn right on to a raised path over silt beds, and go across open heath and into woodland. Continue to reach a minor road. Cross and turn right over a footbridge to reach the car park at the start.

POINTS OF INTEREST:
Kingsbury Water Park – An important recreation and conservation area – 600 acres of old gravel pits with more than 30 lakes and pools. There are good facilities for all kinds of sports, including windsurfing, sailing and fishing. The various activities are accommodated on different lakes so disturbance is kept to a minimum. There is a nature reserve at the northern end with bird hides. Heron, Kingfisher, Common Terns, Great-crested Grebes, Cormorants, Little Ringed Plovers and Lapwings are all possible sightings. Woodland birds include – Siskins, Long-tailed Tits, Greenfinches, Fieldfares, and Redwings. Excellent information leaflets, with detailed maps, are available from the Visitor Centre.
Kingsbury – The church of St Peter and St Paul is of Norman origin, though the tower dates from the 14th century. The village name derives from the 10th-century kings of Mercia who were buried here. The Royal Palace is now part of a farm on private land. Little remains except parts of a hall, archway and walls.

REFRESHMENTS:
Royal Oak Inn, Kingsbury.
The Visitor Centre at the Kingsbury Water Park has a cafe.

Walk 34   **COOMBE ABBEY**   5m (8km)

Maps: OS Sheets Landranger 140; Pathfinder 935, 936, 955 and 956.

Delightful woodlands in a country park, and an easy figure-of-eight ramble on good paths.

Start: At 405795, the Visitor Centre car park, Coombe Abbey.

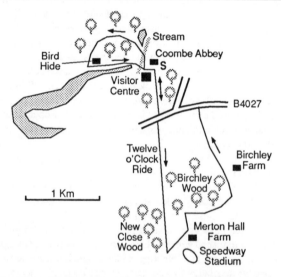

Go past the Visitor Centre and walk towards the lake. At the time of writing, the remains of the abbey on the right are being converted into an hotel. Cross a bridge, then ignore a left turn over another bridge and walk straight on between a stream and some magnificent Redwoods. Turn left at a T-junction by a lake, and then right by some buildings on to a path which circles the edge of the wood, passing to the right of a large pond. Although the path forks, the two paths soon meet again after 100 yards: keep to the main path, with a stream on the right and go over a bridge. Turn right and, at the next fork, follow the **Centenary Way**. Walk down to the next turning and go left, away from the Centenary Way, to follow a path through woodland and a clearing to reach a T-junction. Turn right on a path which skirts the edge of the park for ¹/₂ mile, going through woodland with views over open farmland. The path now swings left at a fence to emerge by a bird hide at the lake. Turn left and walk alongside the lake, crossing a footbridge and, after several hundred yards, go over the bridge passed earlier to return to the car park.

Now walk back to the main road (the B4027), cross, with care, and take the bridleway, called the Twelve o'Clock Ride, which is part of the Centenary Way. Follow the Way between fields to reach a gate into New Close Wood. At the far end of the wood is a sign 'Keep Out – Snakes in Wood!' True or not, the wood is private and you should not stray from the footpath, which can be muddy. Follow the path to a lane and turn left, leaving the Centenary Way which goes to the right.

Just before Merton Hall Farm, turn left through a gate and keep to the left edge of a field. The path swings right, goes through a kissing gate and then turns left. At the top corner of the field, turn right, still with the wood (Birchley Wood this time) on the left, and walk past a long field to reach a gate in the corner, with a pond on the right. The path beyond goes through a corner of the woodland to emerge by a field. Turn left, between a wire fence and a hedgerow, to join the drive to Birchley Farm. Turn left along the drive to reach the main road. Turn left and walk, with care, along the grass verges. Go past a road junction on the right and, shortly, you will come to the main gate of the **Country Park**.

POINTS OF INTEREST:

Centenary Way – Opened in 1989 and using existing rights of way, the Way runs for (surprise, surprise) 100 miles from Kingsbury Water Park in the north of Warwickshire to Meon Hill in the south.

Coombe Abbey Country Park – The Park was opened in 1966 and comprises 280 acres of beautiful woodland, with several lakes and formal gardens. The Abbey was a Cistercian Monastery, founded in 1150. After the Dissolution, it was incorporated into a private house and was the seat of the Earls of Craven until 1923. In the early 1600s, it was the home of Princess Elizabeth, daughter of James I, who married Frederick, Elector of the Palatinate, and became the Winter Queen of Bohemia. A hotel is being built on the site of the house. The grounds were landscaped by Capability Brown around 1770 and the Redwoods passed on the walk are at least 125 years old. The woods are an excellent habitat for many birds, including Kestrel, Sparrowhawk, Kingfisher, and a wide range of woodland species particularly Warblers. Foxes, Deer, Stoats and Hedgehogs are among the mammals which thrive here. The lake is home to one of the largest heronries in Warwickshire, overlooked by a hide.

REFRESHMENTS:

There are several cafes in the Visitor Centre and many picnic tables.

Walk 35   SHUSTOKE AND NETHER WHITACRE   5m (8km)

Maps: OS Sheets Landranger 139; Pathfinder 914.
Fields, reservoirs and several fine villages.
Start: At 227909, the centre of Shustoke village.

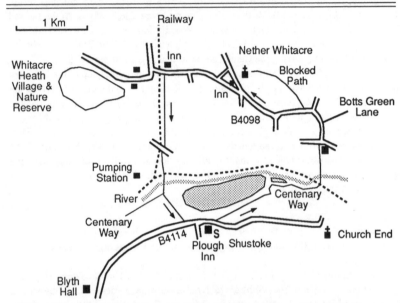

Go down Bixhill Lane, opposite the Plough Inn in **Shustoke**, and follow the Centenary Way along a tarmac lane and the edge of a field to reach a stile on the left. Go over on to a permissive path (part of the Centenary Way) around the southern side of the smaller reservoir. At the right-hand corner, go over stiles and turn left beside the river. Go under a railway bridge, then ignore the Centenary Way and head slightly left to cross a footbridge. Take the path on the left, go over a stile and climb a pasture to reach another stile. Go over and follow the hedge on the left to the stile before the house. Go over and turn right, along the field edge, to a gateway. Go right, and, shortly, left into Botts Green Lane, turning left at the first junction.

Soon, a stile on the right is reached. Although a path is marked on the map across fields to **Nether Whitacre**, the path disappears at the next field corner. There is no clear route visible and no way through the hedgerows in the fields beyond.

Unfortunately this is a common problem in Warwickshire and any such difficulty should be reported to the local council and the Ramblers Association. Until the way is re-opened, keep to the minor road, turning right on to the B4098, past a garden centre, and going right at the next junction, by an inn, to reach Nether Whitacre. Go past the lane to the church to reach a crossroads. Turn left, and at the next junction, right again towards **Whitacre Heath**. Just before the railway bridge, turn left to rejoin the Centenary Way, walking beside the railway. After passing a footbridge over the railway the path swings left across a field. Go over a footbridge and continue to cross a double stile. Turn right along the edge of a field, switching sides halfway along. Follow the hedge on the left to rejoin the path by the railway. Cross a road bridge, turn left and, immediately, right over a stile. Go along a field edge, crossing a stile halfway along. The path beyond leads along the railway embankment to a stile by the main-line railway, with Nether Whitacre pumping station on the right. Cross the railway with care to the stile on the far side. Go over and turn right, along the field edge to a marker post. The path now heads slightly left to reach a footbridge, beyond which a partly-surfaced path crosses fields and stiles to reach the B4114. Turn left, with care, to return to the start.

POINTS OF INTEREST:
Shustoke – The reservoirs, fed by the River Bourne, supply water to storage reservoirs at Coventry and Nuneaton. The grassland surrounding the water blooms with daisies, buttercups and speedwell in the summer. Nearby Blythe Hall was the 17th-century home of Sir William Dugdale, a great historian of the area. St Cuthbert's Church lies at Church End, a mile from the present village because plague forced villagers away from the original site around the church.
Nether Whitacre – St Giles' Church has a part 14th-century chancel and a 16th-century sandstone tower studded with carved faces. The Victorian pumping station once housed James Watt's steam engines, now in the Birmingham Science Museum.
Whitacre Heath – Outside the village, by the River Tame, is a Nature Reserve managed by the Warwickshire Wildlife Trust. It is open only to Trust members. Over the years, 200 plants and grasses, 22 types of butterfly and 122 bird species have been recorded, making this a valuable conservation area.

REFRESHMENTS:
The Plough Inn, Shustoke.
The Dog Inn, Nether Whitacre.
The Gate, Nether Whitacre.
The Swan Inn, Whitacre Heath.

HARBURY 5m (8km)
or 7m (11km)

Maps: OS Sheets Landranger 151; Pathfinder 998.
A striking windmill and lovely church.
Start: At 374598, Park Lane, Harbury.

As part of this walk is along tarmac lanes, it is ideal for winter when footpaths may be
waterlogged.

From the village hall, go left along Park Lane out of **Harbury**. After the road
swings left, uphill, go left along the drive to Whitegates Farm. Go over a stile, through
a gateway and ahead, over two stiles, into a field. Cross to a stile on to Beggar's Lane.
Turn right to a junction. Continue ahead, then go left down a minor road. The short
detour to **Chesterton Windmill** is recommended, particularly for the views. Continue
down the road and turn first left, signed to Chesterton Green. Ignore a right turn and
continue along the road to **Chesterton** Church.

The shorter route turns left through the churchyard to a gate. Cross a stile and a
footbridge ahead, then climb the slope towards Humble Bee cottages, once part of the

stables of Peyto mansion. The brick wall nearby formed part of the kitchen garden. Go over a stile, past the cottages and across fields, switching sides of the hedge at a gap, to reach a gate. Cross a road to a stile and bridge, and keep to the right edge of several fields, crossing stiles and another bridge to reach Park Lane by Temple House. Turn right to reach the start.

The longer route continues past the church, with the first of many lakes on the right. Walk along the estate road of Kingston Manor, passing the house before turning right on to a farm road at a T-junction. Descend, with lakes on either side, then climb a tree-lined avenue to swing left in front of Kingston Farm. Although the bridleway on the map turns left across fields, the landowner prefers the estate roads to be used: follow the road, turning left, then right past Kingston Barn. Go past a conifer plantation to reach a junction with a private drive. Turn left through the double gates and keep to the right edge of the next fields, going through two gates and passing Harbury Heath to reach a gate on to a road. Turn right, but soon go over a stile in the hedge opposite. Go over another stile and keep the hedge on your right to reach a stile on to Bush Heath Lane. Turn right, and almost immediately left over a stile to briefly join the Centenary Way. Cross a field to a stile in the corner of a fence. Turn right along the edge of playing fields and go over another stile. Turn left and go over another stile, passing behind allotments to reach Park Lane.

POINTS OF INTEREST:
Harbury – The Wagstaffe School, founded in 1611, was in use until the 1960s. It was built by Jane Wagstaffe, whose memorial is in the 13th-century All Saints' Church. The Natural History Museum has a collection of local fossils.
Chesterton Windmill – The windmill was commissioned by Sir Edward Peyto in 1632 and is attributed to Inigo Jones. The existing machinery, restored in the late 1960s, dates from 1860 and was last used in 1910. The windmill, as well as being both structurally and mechanically unique, is a striking landmark for miles around.
Chesterton – A fortified manor house, built by the Peyto family, once stood behind the church. The Peyto line ended in 1746 and, following an earlier marriage, the manor and estate passed to the Compton Verney family. The manor was demolished in 1802. A gateway, built in 1630 and restored in 1988, was the private entrance to the churchyard from the manor house. The interior of the 12th-century St Giles' Church, restored in 1862, is full of interest with monuments to the Peyto family including the hand-painted tomb of Humphrey Peyto.

REFRESHMENTS:
There is a good choice of inns in Harbury.

Walk 38 SALTWELLS WOOD AND NETHERTON HILL 5m (8km)

Maps: OS Sheets Landranger 139; Pathfinder 933.

A varied Black Country walk. Plenty of industrial archaeology and natural history interest.

Start: At 934868, the car park at Saltwells Nature Reserve.

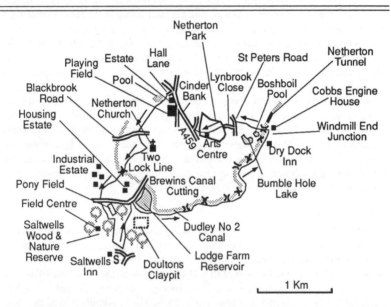

Enter **Saltwells Nature Reserve** by the information board and take the path ahead, passing Doulton's Claypit to reach a road. Turn immediately right up steps and right again alongside **Lodge Farm Reservoir**. Go through the Yacht Club car park and turn right along the towpath of the Dudley No. 2 canal. The canal was built in the 1790s and, although not the most picturesque stretch of canal in the Midlands, it is remarkable for its birdlife. Follow the towpath for $1\frac{1}{2}$ miles to reach the Toll End Works bridges and Cobbs Engine House in a surprisingly rural setting at Windmill End.

Go left over the bridge just before Netherton Tunnel and take the main path, with the delightfully named Bumble Hole Lake (a former claypit) and Boshboil Pool off to the left. The latter, where only the central island of oxidised slag remains of the furnaces and coke ovens, teems with dragonflies. Follow a narrow lane alongside

68

railings to St Peter's Road and turn left. After 100 yards, turn right down **Lynbrook Close**. Now watch for a path on the left into **Netherton Park**. Follow the main path, passing to the right of the Arts Centre to reach the A459 (Cinder Bank). Cross, with care, and turn right along the road. Go past a playing field and Corbetts estate, then turn left down Hall Lane into Saltwells Reserve.

Follow the path to the left of the pool and cross Blackbrook Road. (A diversion left, uphill, to Netherton Church is recommended if only for the fine views.) Head downhill across the gorse-covered hillside towards the canal and the two bridges at Two Lock Line. Off to the left is Brewins Canal section, a deep cutting where the exposed Carboniferous and Silurian rocks are over 260 million years old. Cross the right-hand bridge, walk ahead and then go left along a lower path, crossing the bridge ahead. Go left on a path parallel to the industrial estate, cross a road and go up the steps opposite into a wood. Keep ahead, then turn left by a fallen tree and seat, and immediately bear right at a fork. Join a gravel path, then turn left along the top end of Pony Field to reach a path junction. Turn right up the path by wooden railings next to a pool to join another path. Turn left at another path junction, going past a gate to reach the starting car park.

POINTS OF INTEREST:
Saltwells Nature Reserve – The Reserve took its name from a famous 17th-century salt spa. Over the years the area has been exploited for coal, clay and salt. Since 1981 the land has been a Nature Reserve, one of the largest situated wholly within an urban area and is a remarkable wildlife oasis. Consisting mainly of oak, sycamore and beech, the wood is home to an incredible variety of wildlife. Breeding birds include wood warblers, great spotted and green woodpeckers, tawny owl, whitethroat and goldcrests and it is a nationally important site for dragonflies with 18 species recorded. Doulton's Claypit was used by the Royal Doulton Company but extraction stopped in the 1940s. Due to the importance of the wildflowers, and particularly orchids, that have colonised the sides and floor of the old pit, it has been declared an SSSI.
Lodge Farm Reservoir – This was a claypit in 1838, and was then used as a top up reservoir for the canal. It is now a popular venue for sailing, fishing and birdwatching.
Netherton Park – Netherton was once the centre of a nail, anchor and chain making industry. Netherton Hill was mined for coal in the 1960s and reclaimed in 1973. St Andrew's Church was built in the 1820s by Thomas Lee.

REFRESHMENTS:
Saltwells Inn, at the start.
The Dry Dock Inn, Windmill End.

Walk 39   CUBBINGTON AND HUNNINGHAM   5m (8km)

Maps: OS Sheets Landranger 151; Pathfinder 976.

Three interesting churches are visited on this enjoyable walk.

Start: At 344685, Church Lane, Cubbington.

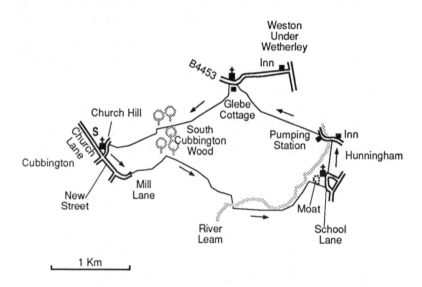

Parking is limited on Church Lane, so please show consideration to residents. Alternative parking is possible in the lay-by on the B4453 in Weston under Wetherley.

Walk past the church, across Church Hill and down New Street, continuing into Mill Lane. At a bend, swing left and follow a sunken lane to its end. Now follow the hedge on the left to pass the southern edge of South Cubbington Wood. Follow the hedge on the left across two fields, go through a gap at the corner and straight across the field beyond. On reaching a fence, bear right, down through a hollow and cross a footbridge over the River Leam. Ignore a path to the right, crossing to the fence ahead and turning left, with the fence on your right. At the end of the field, switch sides of the fence, walking parallel to the river. Maintain direction across the next field, then follow the hedge on the right to a stile by a gate. Go over and turn right, passing a moated site and crossing a field to reach School Lane. Turn left to the church in **Hunningham** and take the path on its right. Cross a field and a ditch, walking parallel to the river to reach the road by Hunningham Bridge.

Turn left, over the bridge, and, just past a pumping station, turn left over a fence. Ignore a path going left and head uphill, keeping the hedge on your left to reach the corner of a copse. Cross into the field on the right and follow the hedge on the left across the field beyond. Follow the hedge on the right across the next field, and at its end go diagonally right up another field to its top left corner. Go through a gate and follow the hedge on the right to the B4453 in **Weston under Wetherley**. The inn is further down the road to the right. Turn left and, just after Glebe Cottage, go left into a field. Follow the hedge on the left, then walk straight across the next field to a footbridge. Cross and turn right along the bottom of the field, crossing a track near Weston Hall. Now follow the hedge on the left, crossing a redundant footbridge and two fields. Bear slightly right to a path into, and through, South Cubbington Wood. Turn left down the edge of the field beyond, then swing right along the edge of next field. Go over a footbridge and follow the left side of the field beyond to reach the corner by houses. Turn left to reach Church Hill in **Cubbington**.

POINTS OF INTEREST:

Hunningham – The 13th-century St Margaret's Church was built by the Corbucion family who also owned the manor. A pauper asylum was sited in Hunningham House in 1846, but closed in 1850 following allegations of ill-treatment of the inmates. The house is now privately owned. Nearby is a medieval moated site and a massive arched bridge, partly rebuilt in 1651.

Weston under Wetherley – Weston hospital was built in 1840 as a reformatory for boys. St Michael's Church boasts one of the oldest brasses in the county, commemorating Anne Dunet and dated 1497.

Cubbington – St Mary's Church has a Norman tower and font. Inside is a memorial to Abraham Murcott, a sailor who lost his life when his ship sank off the Isles of Scilly. The churchyard is managed for wildlife, with bird and bat boxes. One rector was James, the brother of Jane Austen, who lived here from 1792 to 1820.

REFRESHMENTS:
The Red Lion, Hunningham.
The King's Head, Cubbington.
The Bull Inn, Weston under Wetherley – slightly off the route.

Walk 40   LONG LAWFORD AND NEWBOLD ON AVON   5m (8km)
Maps: OS Sheets Landranger 140; Pathfinder 956.
A charming walk across farmland and through a mini canal tunnel to a Nature Reserve.
Start: At 474764, Long Lawford Church.

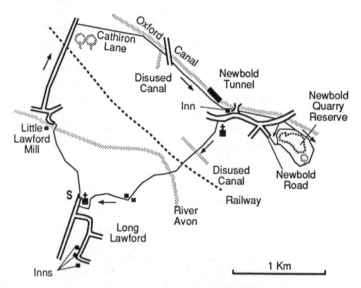

Parking is limited by the church; please park sympathetically.

Go through a metal gate by a fingerpost and follow a bridleway between fences and through another gate. Follow the hedge on the right, cross a causeway and footbridge over the River Avon and go through a gate by Little Lawford Mill. Turn left following a lane to a T-junction. Turn left and, shortly, right along the Harborough Magna road. Cross a railway and, by a lay-by at the end of trees, turn right along a track (Cathiron Lane) to reach the canal Bridge 44. Climb down to the Oxford Canal towpath (*see* Note to Walk 8) and turn right. Cross a wrought iron bridge spanning an arm of the canal abandoned when cuttings and embankments were constructed to shorten the canal by over 13 miles. Walk under two bridges and enter Newbold tunnel. Although from a distance the tunnel appears short, it becomes very dark in the middle and a torch will save you from wet feet! Look for the stalactite columns and curtains hanging from the ceiling. There is a single handrail, but please keep children and dogs under control. Continue past the inn, go under Green Bridge and, at a gap on the right, by an information board, enter the **Newbold on Avon** Reserve. Both the left and right-hand paths circle the pool: choose either and head for the top right corner.

Go down the lane onto Newbold Road. Turn right, go over a crossroads and uphill to the church. Go through the churchyard, over a stile and follow a path through an avenue of trees. Cross a footbridge over the bed of an abandoned canal (a continuation of the canal arm passed earlier) and go along the tarmac path to a lane. Go under the railway bridge, then right through a kissing gate and cross a footbridge. Go up the meadow to a stile and straight across the next two fields to reach an alleyway behind houses. Turn right along the alleyway, cross a green and turn left. Soon, turn right between Nos. 45 and 47. Go straight over the field beyond, cross a footbridge and bear half-left to a metal gate to the left of the house. Go along a path and turn right through the churchyard to return to **Long Lawford**.

POINTS OF INTEREST:

Long Lawford – The lands surrounding the village were once owned by the Benedictine order of Monks Kirby. The old churchyard of St John's Church was overgrown for many years, but was cleared by local volunteers in 1991. The hedge has been relaid, trees and shrubs planted and over 500 wildflowers sown. Bat and bird boxes have also been provided.

Newbold on Avon – Since 1993 Newbold Quarry Park has been managed by the Warwickshire Wildlife Trust in partnership with Rugby Council. The quarry was worked for limestone until the 1920's and was then used as a top-up reservoir for the Oxford Canal. One quarry face is still visible high above the pool. The park and lake support a wide range of wildlife including the rare crayfish. Great crested grebe, moorhen, and coot are among the many wildfowl seen on the lake. Flowers including wild strawberry, blue fleabane, wild parsnip, fairy flax and milkworth thrive. St Botolph's red sandstone church dates mostly from the 15th century and contains a Jacobean communion table and an early 18th-century wrought iron tower screen.

REFRESHMENTS:

There are numerous possibilities in both Long Lawford and Newbold on Avon.

Walk 41   BULKINGTON AND MARSTON JABBETT   5m (8km)

Maps: OS Sheets Landranger 140; Pathfinder 935.

A circuit across farmland and along canal towpaths. The paths can be overgrown in summer.

Start: At 392867, Bulkington Church.

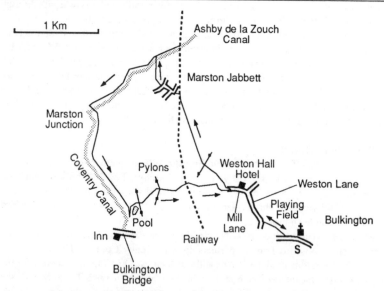

With the church on your right, walk along the road and across the playing fields to join an alleyway through a housing estate. This emerges on to Weston Lane: turn right, passing the school, then turn left down Mill lane (in front of the **Weston Hall Hotel**). Where the houses end, go over a stile on the right. (Notice the 'Your Green Track' signs, a marvellous initiative by Nuneaton and Bedworth council to maintain and publicise footpaths in the area. Despite this, there are still problems with some footpaths being overgrown by crops, particularly in summer. Shorts are not recommended – unless you save the walk for another time of year!)

From the stile, go half-right across the field, passing the corner of another hedge to reach the bottom corner of the field. Go through a gap and follow the hedge on the right to reach a stile by a house. Walk ahead along the lane beyond, going under a railway line to reach a road junction in **Marston Jabbett**. Continue ahead, ignoring a left turn and bearing right along the road to a T-junction. Turn left and, shortly, right over a stile. Go straight across a field, cross another stile and head for the canal bridge ahead. Turn left along the towpath of the **Ashby de la Zouch Canal** to reach Marston Junction at Marston Bridge. Turn left over the bridge on to the Coventry Canal (*see* Note to Walks 23 & 24) and walk south along the towpath for a mile to reach a large gap in the hedge on the left, by a pool. (The Navigation Inn lies further down the canal at Bulkington Bridge).

Leave the canal, cross the footbridge and stile and skirt the field on the left edge of the pool. The path follows the field edge under a line of pylons (it should cross the field diagonally left, but there is no trace of it on the ground). Turn left at the field corner and follow the hedge on the right under another line of pylons to reach a farm track by a house. Go straight over and continue to cross a railway line via a bridge. Follow the hedge on the right (if crops permit) across a long field to reach a gate on to Mill lane. Turn left to rejoin the outward route, reversing it to **Bulkington**.

POINTS OF INTEREST:

Weston Hall Hotel – The manor house is 16th-century, although a house is believed to have been on the site since the 13th century. The manor retains Elizabethan gables on the south front and is now a hotel.

Marston Jabbett – This was once a densely populated area of Bulkington but is now just a few isolated houses. The original name was Merston, meaning 'marshy' as the area was once low-lying and wet. The modern name is partly derived from the 14th-century Jabbett family.

Ashby de la Zouch Canal – The canal was opened in 1804 and is completely lock-free. It is 22 miles long and meets the Coventry Canal at Marston Junction. Plants which may be seen include reed sweet-grass, water plantain, reedmace, great willowherb, hard rush and sedges.

Bulkington – St James' Church tower was built in the late 14th century. Inside are a marble font and monuments to the Hayward family dating from the late 18th century.

REFRESHMENTS:
The White Lion, Bulkington.
The Rule and Compass, Bulkington.
The Navigation Inn, near the canal.

Walk 42   WOODGATE VALLEY   5m (8km)

Maps: OS Sheets Landranger 139; Pathfinder 933 and 934. The Birmingham A-Z is also useful.

A gentle urban ramble in the Bournbrook valley: through a Country Park to castle ruins.

Start: At 995829, Woodgate Valley Country Park Visitor Centre.

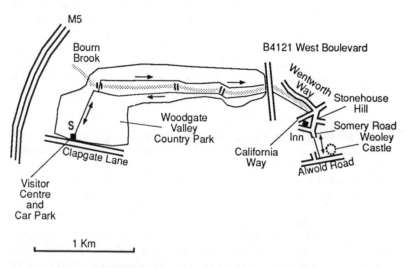

This walk is linear, with a return almost along the same route and offers an ideal introduction to the Country Park's wildlife with a slice of history thrown in. Make sure you visit when the castle ruins and museum are open. At present that is March to October, Tuesday to Friday, afternoons only – tel: 0121 427 4270.

Go past the Visitor Centre and a wooden barrier, where fine views open out across the entire park. Such a rural scene comes as a surprise as the valley is hidden from view from the car park. Walk down the path between horse paddocks, then keep ahead across grass to reach the footbridge over Bourn Brook. Although the walk follows the main path each side of the brook, do not miss exploring the rest of the park. The other paths are quieter and birdwatchers, in particular, will be richly rewarded. A detailed map and leaflets are available from the Visitor Centre.

Turn right along the main gravel path beside the brook, passing two bridges, and walking for nearly two miles to reach the end of the park. Cross the busy B4121 (West Boulevard) with care and continue beside the brook, going between houses to emerge on to California Way. Go straight over and walk up Stonehouse Hill to the Somery Road junction. At the end of Somery Road take an alleyway which leads over the old canal to Alwold Road. **Weoley Castle** is on the left. After your visit, retrace the outward route to cross West Boulevard and re-enter **Woodgate Valley Country Park**. Now take the path on the left, with Bourn Brook on your right. Once again all the side paths are worth exploring. As with all Country Parks close to housing, the usual problems with vandalism and litter are in evidence, although thankfully the problem is not too widespread. When you reach the first footbridge crossed on the outward journey, turn left, uphill, between the paddocks to return to the Visitor Centre.

POINTS OF INTEREST:

Weoley Castle – This large, moated manor house in the valley of Stonehouse Brook, was built on the site of a previous manor in the 13th Century by Roger de Somery. A later owner, William Berkeley, supported Richard III at Bosworth Field. After the King's death, the manor was given to the Dudleys, who in turn sold it to Richard Jerveys. The existing remains consist mainly of the walls.

Woodgate Valley Country Park – The efforts of local residents and conservation trusts prevented the development of this area into factories and the 450 acres were created a Country Park in 1984. A programme of hedge replanting has begun with hawthorn, hazel, honeysuckle, ivy, bluebells, foxgloves thriving in the newly created habitats. Although close to an urban area, the woodland, numerous ponds and meadows are home to a rich diversity of wildlife: 280 species of plants and wildflowers have so far been recorded. Foxes, voles, stoats and weasels find a safe haven, and migrant birds such as cuckoo, chiffchaff, willow warbler and whitethroat can be seen along with rarer visitors such as wheatear, garden warbler and blackcap. Skylarks, meadow pipits, kestrels, sparrowhawks and little owls have bred successfully and in wetland areas kingfisher, grey wagtail, snipe and heron are found. Hole Farm and its pony trekking centre is open to visitors. A programme of school visits, guided walks and lectures takes place throughout the year.

REFRESHMENTS:

The Stonehouse Inn, Stonehouse Lane.
There is a cafe at the Visitor Centre.

Maps: OS Sheets Landranger 139; Pathfinder 954, 955, 975 and 976.

Farmland and a canal feature on this enjoyable, easy walk.
Start: At 206706, the car park, Hay Wood.

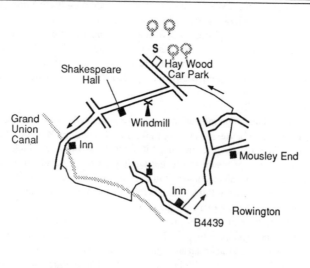

Parking is very limited in Rowington. The inn car parks are for patrons only and the church car park is private. Because of this, the walk starts from Hay Wood car park.

From Hay Wood, turn left down the lane and go right at the first junction. Walk past a converted windmill (now a private house) and Shakespeare Hall, on the left, to reach a crossroads with the B4439. Cross straight over and continue along the lane opposite to reach an inn and the Grand Union Canal (*see* Note to Walk 5). Turn left along the towpath, following it for a mile to reach the next bridge (Rowington Hill Bridge). Leave the canal here, walking up the track to emerge opposite the church.

Turn right down the B4439 and walk through **Rowington** village. Just past the inn, and before the stream, go through a gate on the left. The path beyond leads to the top left corner of the field: go over a stile and a plank bridge and turn right to follow the hedge on the right. Go over a stile on to a lane. Turn left, uphill, along the lane and then right along Case Lane, signed to Mousley End. Go past the entrance to Mousley House Farm and turn left over a stile. Follow the footpath beyond straight across the field. Follow the hedge on the right in the field beyond to reach a lane.

Turn left, and almost immediately right, over a stile. Follow the hedge on the left to reach a stile. Go over and turn left along the left edge of the field to reach a stile by a gateway. Now follow the hedge on the left to reach a stile and footbridge in the corner. In the huge field beyond, head half-left to the top corner and go through a gate on to a lane. Turn right up the lane to return to the car park.

POINTS OF INTEREST:

Rowington – This beautiful village unfortunately suffers from heavy through traffic. In more tranquil days, during the late 11th century, a community of Cistercian nuns was founded in a Priory here by the Abbot of Reading. Following the Dissolution, the priory and surrounding lands were sold to William Wigston. The privately owned Shakespeare Hall is thought to have connections with the Shakespeare family, the name first appearing in parish registers in 1485. It is claimed that a previous occupant, Thomas Shakespeare, was William Shakespeare's uncle. St Lawrence's Church stands in a beautiful setting on a hilltop and has a 14th-century tower, a 15th-century pulpit, a restored chancel and a Perpendicular west window.

REFRESHMENTS:
The Cock Horse Inn, Rowington.
The Tom o' the Wood, Turners Green.

Walk 44   KINVER EDGE AND KINGSFORD   5$\frac{1}{2}$m (9km)

Maps: OS Sheets Landranger 138; Pathfinder 933.

A wonderful ridge walk with extensive views, past old cave dwellings. Good paths.

Start: At 846834, in High Street, Kinver.

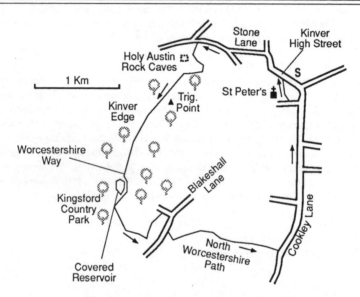

Walk west along the High Street, past Vicarage Drive, to the end of the village. Turn left into Stone Lane and climb for $\frac{1}{2}$ mile until trees appear on the left. Here, turn left through a handgate and go uphill, with the rock houses of Holy Austin Rock on the right. At a crossroads, take the path, left, up wooden steps to reach a grassy shoulder. Turn right and climb steeply up steps to the top of the Iron Age fort. On a clear day the views from here include the Welsh and Shropshire hills as well as much of the Midlands. Turn left and follow the ridge top path, ignoring any side paths and a grassy spur on the left. Descend slightly, passing a brick building. Go across at a junction and continue to the trig. point. Continue through trees and a wooden barrier to reach an information board and the junction of three long distance footpaths: the Staffordshire Way, the Worcestershire Way and the North Worcestershire Path.

Keep straight ahead, entering **Kingsford Country Park**, following the Worcestershire Way. When the path forks, take the left branch, downhill, still on the Way, passing a covered reservoir on the right. At the bottom of the hill the Way goes right, but you turn left along a bridleway, parallel with a grassy path and woods on the left. At the next junction, ignore a right turn, going straight on, still on the bridleway. After a footpath joins from the left, cross another waymarked route and, on nearing houses, turn left to walk between woods and houses. At a T-junction, turn right and then go right again into Blakeshall Lane. After 100 yards, take the North Worcestershire Path, on the left. The route swings left, and then left again along an enclosed bridleway. Continue along the Path between fields to reach Cookley Lane. Turn left along the road, (towards Kinver) ignoring side roads, for 1 mile. On reaching a dangerous S-bend, turn left into Church Road, signed to **Kinver Edge**. Walk uphill and take the first turn right into St Peter's churchyard, at the rear of which is a signed path which leads steeply downhill. The path is eroded and slippery and requires care. Go straight over at a junction of four paths and keep ahead along a narrow alleyway which leads into **Kinver** High Street.

POINTS OF INTEREST:

Kingsford Country Park – The Park is 200 acres of heath, sandstone outcrops and woodland, with commercial plantations of Larch, Scots and Corsican Pine. Fungi such as the scarlet and white fly agaric thrive.

Kinver Edge – Now in the care of the National Trust, the friable, sandstone ridge has a warren of caves and hollows and the remains of an Iron Age fort. The cave dwellings were populated in the Middle Ages by hermits: some houses were still inhabited until the 1950s. Holy Austin Rock and its occupants feature in 19th-century photographs and the words 'Rock House Cafe' can still be seen on one of the walls, although the cafe closed in 1967.

Kinver – St Peter's Church is perched high above the bustling village. Foley Chapel was built around 1445 by John Hampton, Lord of Kinver. He was Esquire of the Body to Henry VI and was endowed with many grants of properties and offices, losing those gifts during the Wars of the Roses. After his death, in 1472, Kinver was given to Clarence, brother of Edward IV, and then to Tewkesbury Abbey, being reclaimed in 1485 by Henry VII and eventually passing to the Foley family.

REFRESHMENTS:

There is a good choice of inns and cafes in Kinver.

Walk 45　TANWORTH IN ARDEN AND UMBERSLADE　5½m (9km)

Maps: OS Sheets Landranger 139; Pathfinder 954.

An attractive walk through parkland and fields. Well waymarked but muddy.

Start: At 113705, the village green, Tanworth.

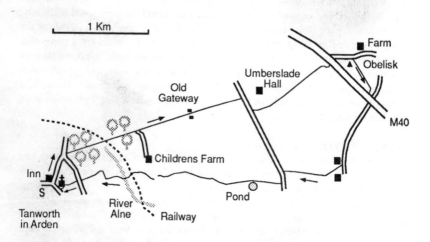

Walk down the lane past the school, with the church on your right. At the junction, take the lane ahead, signed to Children's Farm. There is no mistaking the correct path as the lane passes through a magnificent avenue of poplar trees which once linked the estate of **Umberslade Hall** and the village. Go under the railway and, when the lane swings right, stay on the muddy path uphill, passing through a derelict gateway. Head towards the Hall to reach a road.

Turn right, and, shortly, take the fenced path on the left, going through a metal gate at its end. Walk with the fence on your left across two fields, go through a metal gate and over the stile and footbridge ahead. Go under the M40, cross another stile and turn right up a lane. Opposite the farm, go over a stile on the right and walk to the left of the obelisk. Go past a barn and keep the hedge on your left to reach a stile at the top left corner of the field. Go over the stile and a footbridge on to a green lane. Turn right, and shortly left, up steps. Turn right to cross the M42, continuing down the lane for $^{1}/_{2}$ mile, past houses, to reach a gate on the right, by a marker post. Go through and take the path beyond, going straight ahead and then swinging left before a metal gate. Go around a field edge to reach a stile by a pond. Go over and turn right, walking with a fence on your left, to reach another stile. Go over and walk straight ahead, passing a power pole to reach a road.

Turn left, and shortly right through a gateway to go along a rutted lane. Go through a gap and keep ahead along a line of trees, passing a pond. Now follow the hedge on your left across a long field. At the end, turn right, and shortly left over a footbridge and stile. Continue ahead, ignoring a path to the left, across a field and then follow the hedge on the right to reach a gap, also on the right. Do not go through the gap: instead, turn left, and then right along the field edge to reach a metal gate. Go through and turn half-left through another gate. Now follow the hedge on your left until you are halfway across the field (by a marker post), then turn right past a line of trees to reach a stile by the Children's Farm. Go over and turn left under the railway. Go over a stile and cross a footbridge. Keep to the left edge of the field beyond to reach a stile. Go over and walk with a hedge on your right, switching sides halfway along to go over a stile on to a road. Turn right, then shortly left, uphill, to the churchyard in **Tanworth in Arden**.

POINTS OF INTEREST:

Umberslade Hall – The Hall was originally built, in 1680, on the site of a moated manor house by Andrew Archer. It remained the home of the Archer family for over six centuries. Thomas Archer was responsible for designing and building Birmingham Cathedral. To commemorate becoming a Baron, Thomas Archer built an obelisk in the grounds in 1749. The Hall was occupied by troops in World War II and is now converted into private apartments.

Tanworth in Arden – Originally a clearing in the Forest of Arden, this unspoilt village has attractive timber-framed houses and many Georgian buildings. The neat village green and seat is conveniently near the inn. The 14th-century church of St Mary Magdelene houses monuments to the Archer family. The spire, which dominates the landscape, was rebuilt in 1720. The stone slab lintel over the window in the south side of the tower possibly comes from old coffin lids. A previous vicar was the Reverend Phillip Wren, great grandson of the architect.

REFRESHMENTS:
The Bell Inn, Tanworth in Arden.

Walk 46   OVERSLEY GREEN AND WIXFORD   5$\frac{1}{2}$m (9km)

Maps: OS Sheets Landranger 150; Pathfinder 997.

Fine views and a charming church are features of this enjoyable walk.

Start: At 091575, High Street, Alcester.

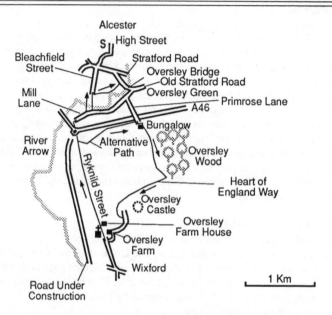

From the High Street, head south to cross the Stratford Road. Go down Bleachfield Street, turning left over a stile opposite No. 95. Follow the hedge on the right across pasture, switching sides in the next meadow to walk alongside the River Arrow for a few yards. Now bear left to the sports field and follow the hedge on the right to reach the old Stratford Road. Turn right over Oversley bridge, built in 1600, and then right again down Mill Lane in Oversley Green. Turn left down Primrose Lane, joining the Heart of England Way (*see* Note to Walk 66). Cross the A46 via the footbridge and turn left along a bridleway. Go past a bungalow, through a gate and walk uphill along a tarmac lane. By the house at the end, go through a gate on the right and skirt the edge of Oversley Wood along a muddy bridleway.

84

At the corner of the wood, leave the bridleway and turn right along a path between hedges. Keep left when the path rejoins the Heart of England Way, passing an entrance to Oversley Castle. At the next junction go left. This path swings left and climbs, with lovely views over the Cotswolds and Bredon Hill. On reaching the drive to Oversley Castle, turn right, downhill, along an avenue of laburnum trees. Go past Oversley Farm to reach a crossroads by **Wixford** Church. The village and its inns are down the lane to the left. Turn right up a bridleway, passing Oversley Farm House and joining the Roman Ryknild Street to walk along field edges and between trees, crossing two farm tracks. At the time of writing, a road was under construction in the Arrow valley on the left, so the peace of this little corner may soon be lost.

After a mile, you will reach a handgate near the A46. The bridleway crosses the A46 – take great care – and continues to reach Mill Lane. Turn right, then take a path on the left, just beyond the entrance to the caravan site. Cross the river to reach Bleachfield Street, rejoining the outward route which is reversed back to the start.

At the time of writing, roadworks made crossing the A46 difficult, forcing walkers to turn right before the handgate, taking a footpath along the field edge. The pasture beyond was occupied by a bull and there were no warning signs at either end of the field, so please be careful. By the time you read this, it is to be hoped that the true route will again be accessible.

POINTS OF INTEREST:
Wixford – This ancient settlement was built on the site of an old ford. The monks of Bordesley established a fishery here in 1287. The 11th-century church of St Milburgas is set apart from the village and almost hidden behind an enormous yew which was already old in 1669. When the priest attempted to cut it down, the parishioners appealed to the Bishop to prevent him. In the corner of the churchyard is a small, thatched building, possibly dating from the 17th century, once used as a stable for the rector's horse. The chief treasure of the church lies inside the south chapel, where a beautifully preserved brass, constructed in 1411, surmounts the tomb of Thomas Crewe and his wife.

REFRESHMENTS:
The Fish Inn, Wixford.
The Three Horseshoes, Wixford.
There is also plenty of choice in Alcester.

Walk 47   BUBBENHALL AND WAPPENBURY   5¹/₂m (9km)

Maps: OS Sheets Landranger 140 and 151; Pathfinder 955 and 976.

Two delightful woodlands and a charming village.

Start: At 364723, the A445 lay-by near the school in Bubbenhall.

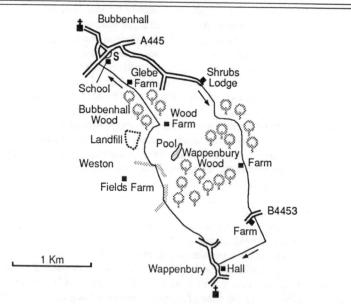

Turn right from the lay-by, passing the village sign, then turn right down Pagets Lane. Go left at the fork, towards Shrubs Lodge, and bear right along a bridleway by the Lodge entrance. Follow the bridleway into the woods – ignore the restricted access notices; you are on a *legal* right of way. On reaching a gravel track, walk ahead, passing a field and a farmhouse. Follow the bridleway ahead through trees to reach a handgate at the far side of the woods. Head straight across the field beyond, go through the right-hand gate (in line with a white house) and follow the hedge on the left to reach a road.

　　Go through the gate opposite and follow the hedge on the right past the buildings. The path now switches into the field on the right and heads downhill to a gate. Go through, turn right and follow the hedge on the right across two fields to another gate.

Follow the hedge on the left in the next field, walking beside Wappenbury Hall to reach a road. The village church lies left and immediately right down the lane. However, the walk turns right to a T-junction. From here to the Woods the paths are poorly defined. Head across a large arable field, to reach the left corner of **Wappenbury Wood**. Continue ahead for 100 yards, then bear left downhill to a footbridge in the far hedge. Cross and turn right along the field edge to reach a stile in the right hedge. Head straight across the next field to another footbridge in the middle of the far hedge. Now turn left along the field edge, keeping hedgerows on your left and passing to the right of a landfill. The paths are not clearly marked, but do not be tempted too far left by the posts and a stile heading towards Weston Fields Farm, south of the landfill: the path leads nowhere and the farmer insists there are no footpaths across his land! If in doubt, head north alongside the hedge towards Bubbenhall Woods: a compass may prove useful to take a precise bearing. Emerging by Wood Farm, follow the marked path through the woods to reach an enclosed track behind Glebe Farm. Turn left and go over a stile at the end of the wood. Cross the field beyond, with the wood on your left, and go over a stile on to a farm drive. Turn left to reach the A445 near **Bubbenhall**: the lay-by is a short way down the road to the right.

POINTS OF INTEREST:
Wappenbury Wood – The wood is owned by the Forestry Commission and leased by the Warwickshire Wildlife Trust. It is home to an amazing variety of butterflies with over 22 species recorded, as well as birds such as nightingale, woodcock, lesser spotted woodpecker and tree pipit. The quiet walker may be rewarded with a glimpse of a muntjac deer. There have been problems in recent years with the owner of the shooting rights in the wood attempting to ban public access. Despite the intimidating notices, this does not affect the legal bridleway running through the woods.

Excavations of an Iron Age earthwork surrounding the village have revealed pottery and the remains of four kilns of the Romano-British period. The village church of St John the Baptist, restored in the 1880s, has beautiful stained glass windows. The 13th-century chancel, nave and south aisle were mostly rebuilt in 1886 when a porch was added. There is an ancient cross in the churchyard. In the 13th century over 250 villagers succumbed to the plague.
Bubbenhall – This was originally known as Bubbas Hill. St Giles' Church has a late 13th-century nave and tower: the east wall was rebuilt in the 19th century.

REFRESHMENTS:
The Malt Shovel, Bubbenhall.

Walk 48 MIDDLE TYSOE AND WINDMILL HILL 5¹/₂m (9km)

Maps: OS Sheets Landranger 151; Pathfinder 1021.

A strenuous walk, with lovely views, to a windmill, returning across fields. Some paths are ill-defined.

Start: At 340443, the main street in Middle Tysoe.

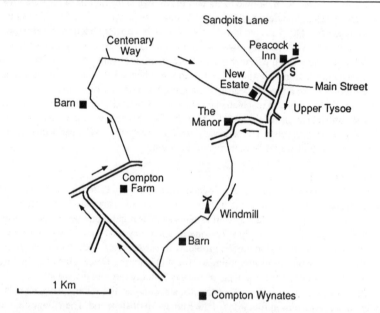

■ Compton Wynates

With the Peacock Inn on your right, walk along the main street through **Middle Tysoe** into Upper Tysoe. At the end of the village, swing right along the Shipston road, then left past The Manor. Shortly after a right-hand bend, go through the first gateway on the left (there are no waymarks) and follow the hedge on the left up **Windmill Hill** to the windmill. **Compton Wynyates** can be seen in the valley on the left. Pass left of the windmill to reach a stile and turn right along the top edge of the field beyond, going through trees to reach another stile. Go over and turn left, going steeply downhill, via new steps. Now follow the fence on the left past an old barn to reach a stile on to a track. Walk ahead to reach a stile by a gate and go down the green lane beyond to reach a lane.

Turn right along the lane, go ahead at a junction and swing right with the road at a T-junction. On the skyline above the buildings on the right can be seen Compton Pike, a stone spire once used as a signal beacon. Walk past Compton Farm's entrance, go over a bridge and turn left along a bridleway. Follow the hedge on the left across four fields until you are level with a barn on the left. The hedges have disappeared so the Pathfinder map is inaccurate here. This, combined with the absence of waymarking and a ploughed up path means route finding can be difficult. Just level with the barn, the path bears half-right across the field and over the crest of the rise to a gate that is not visible until you get nearer. Go through two gates and turn right, following the field edge to join the Centenary Way (*see* Note to Walk 34) at a stile in the hedge. The path should go straight ahead from the last gate and then turn right, but has been ploughed up!

Head across the centre of the pasture to the stile to the left of a gate. Cross a brook by the stepping stones, then leave the Centenary Way, going half-left to reach a stile near the top left corner. Aim for the top left corner of the next field, then follow the hedge on the left to a gap: once again the path is ploughed up. Head for a stile hidden in the top left corner of the field. Go over and aim for the centre of the fence ahead to reach a stile into a new housing estate. The estate is still under construction so paths may change. Walk ahead to a lane and turn left through the new estate to reach a road. Turn right and, shortly, left down Sandpits Lane to reach the main street in Middle Tysoe.

POINTS OF INTEREST:

Middle Tysoe – St Mary's Church contains a 14th-century font, interesting brasses, the remains of a rood loft and an 18th-century bellcote. The figure of a Red Horse, long since vanished, was carved into the hill above the village. Nearby Lower Tysoe, once owned by the Knights Templar, was previously known as Temple Tysoe.

Windmill Hill – The windmill dates from the early 18th century and was worked by the Styles family of Tysoe until the last Styles brother was killed in the First World War. It was restored in the early 1970s by the Marquis of Northampton.

Compton Wynyates – This beautiful mansion nestling in the hills is the home of the Marquis of Northampton, but is no longer open to the public. The home of the Compton family since the 13th century, royal visitors have included Henry VIII, Elizabeth I, James I and Charles I. The mansion was seized and held for a time during the Civil War by Parliamentarians. Despite an attempt to win the house back, it was not until after the war, and on payment of a heavy fine, that the house was returned.

REFRESHMENTS:

The Peacock Inn, Middle Tysoe.

Walk 49 STRATFORD-UPON-AVON AND BORDON HILL   6m (9^1/$_2$km)
Maps: OS Sheets Landranger 151; Pathfinder 997 and 998.
Explore a town packed full of interest, then walk through fields to hill overlooking Stratford.
Start: At 207548, the Tourist Information Centre, Bridgefoot.

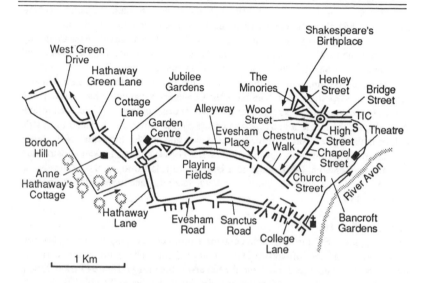

From the Information Centre, **Stratford**, turn right, up Bridge Street, and at the roundabout go half-right up Henley Street towards **Shakespeare's Birthplace**. Opposite the Birthplace, walk down the Minories alleyway, go past the bank and taxi rank, turn left down Wood Street, then right at the roundabout passed earlier, into the High Street. Continue into Chapel Street, passing **New Place** and the Guild Chapel. Go along Church Street past the 15th-century almhouses, on the left, and at the T-junction turn right into Chestnut Walk.

At the next junction, by the traffic lights, go straight across into Evesham Place, and watch for the sign to **Anne Hathaway's Cottage**, leading into an alleyway. This well-marked route crosses three roads, through a residential area, and playing fields to reach Shottery. Go past the garden centre, via the mini-roundabout, and enter Jubilee Gardens, to emerge opposite Anne Hathaway's cottage.

Turn right along Cottage Lane to reach a T-junction. Turn left, and immediately right into Hathaway Green Lane. Now go left into West Green Drive. Almost at the end of the drive, climb a signed stile on the left and cross the centre of the field beyond, heading towards a gap in the hedge ahead. The path can be indistinct across the next two fields: at the gap, look through the centre of the nearest twin telegraph poles, towards a narrow gap in the next hedgerow – aim for this. Climb a stile and walk to the top left-hand corner of the field. Turn left over a stile and cross a narrow footbridge. The line of the path now becomes clearer: after crossing a footbridge, maintain this line over the next four fields, enjoying marvellous views across the town. The church spire is particularly distinctive. Enter a small wood and, at the next path junction, turn left, downhill, passing an orchard on the right. Take the next right fork in the path, which can be muddy. This eventually becomes a gravelled track leading past a wood, on the left, to emerge, after passing a garden centre and school, into Hathaway Lane. Turn right to a T-junction. Turn left on to the busy Evesham Road. After about $\frac{1}{4}$ mile, turn right into Sanctus Road (it has an inn on the corner), passing over a bridge from which there is a closer view of **Holy Trinity Church**. From the church, turn left into Avonbank gardens and follow the delightful riverside path past the theatre and into Bancroft Gardens, opposite the starting point.

POINTS OF INTEREST:

Stratford-upon-Avon – Best visited midweek or out of season to capture the real atmosphere, as it can be very crowded during the Summer. All the Shakespeare properties are worth a visit, whether you are a Shakespeare buff or not, as they also give a flavour of the town's history.

Shakespeare's Birthplace – Shakespeare was born in the western end of the building. The adjoining part was used by his father, John.

New Place – This was purchased by Shakespeare in 1597 when he returned from London. The beautiful, peaceful gardens should not be missed.

Anne Hathaway's Cottage – The approach would have been rather different in the 16th century, entirely over fields. The cottage, which has colourful gardens, was the home of Shakespeare's wife and dates back to the 15th century.

Holy Trinity Church – The church is in an idyllic setting on the riverside and dates from the 13th century. The spire was rebuilt in 1763. The interior has carved choir stalls, a beautiful east window and a bust of Shakespeare, as well as his grave and that of his wife.

REFRESHMENTS:

There is an unlimited choice in Stratford, to suit all tastes and pockets.

Walk 50   **BURTON DASSETT AND FENNY COMPTON**   6m (9¹/₂km)
Maps: OS Sheets Landranger 151; Pathfinder 998 and 999.
An interesting walk through rolling hills to two peaceful villages.
Some paths are not well marked.
Start: At 397519, Burton Dassett Country Park car park.

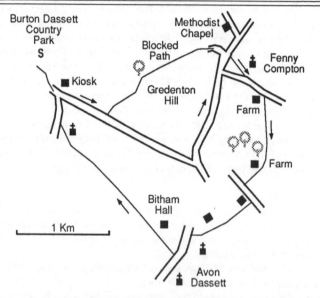

From the **Country Park** car park, go past the entrance kiosk and along the road towards
Fenny Compton. Ignore a right turn to go over a cattle grid, climbing past houses and
a farm. The first, unmarked, gate on the left is the start of a bridleway. (At the time of
writing, the gate was welded shut. The path should go downhill past a wood, skirting
the side of Gredenton Hill, crossing fields to **Fenny Compton**, emerging opposite
Church Street.) Until the way is re-opened, continue along the minor road and turn
left at a crossroads, going downhill to the village. On reaching a seat and the Bear and
Ragged Staff signpost, take the 'No Through Road' half-right. Before the churchyard,
turn right through a gate and cross a field diagonally right to a stile. Turn left, up a
road, past houses and a farm. Just past a slurry tank go right, as waymarked, into a
field, aiming for the trees on the skyline to reach a gate. Climb the slope ahead, going

over a muddy ditch, through two gates and then turning left through an unmarked gate. Walk alongside the hedge and at its end, turn right, past a line of trees and descend towards farm buildings. Turn right, unmarked, into the farmyard, then left, and almost immediately right, to reach a field edge. Turn left, skirting the farm complex to join a drive. Climb the drive to join a minor road, turning left to pass two houses.

Now climb a stile by a gate on the right and cross the field beyond, keeping left of a hollow, to reach a stile. Follow a path inside a fence and through a muddy gateway. At the top of the slope ahead, go over the stile in the corner, turn right along the lane and almost immediately left past a house to emerge behind St John the Baptist Church, **Avon Dassett**. Turn left, through the village, take the lane on the right, before the inn, and pass through a gate with a Centenary Way sign. Continue ahead to reach a gate. Turn right and follow an arrowed path along a field edge. Keeping a hedge on your right, go past a barn and across a muddy ditch and stile. At the next stile is a footbridge with several yellow arrows: go across an arable field to reach a stile with **All Saints' Church** ahead. Three stiles follow in quick succession, the last leading into the churchyard. Walk up the lane, past the site of a Holy Well, over a cattle grid and up the road to regain the car park.

POINTS OF INTEREST:
Burton Dassett Country Park – The hills were designated an SSSI in 1973. At a height of 630 feet, they offer wonderful views. The Beacon was built in the late 14th century by Sir Edward Belknap and became part of the beacon warning system. A wooden post windmill stood alongside in the 1600s, but was blown down in 1946 and never rebuilt. In 1908, on Pleasant Hill, a Saxon burial place holding 35 skeletons was discovered. The hollows are the remains of iron ore quarries from the mid 1800s.
Fenny Compton – Don't miss the tiny Methodist Chapel. Bullet holes in the north door of St Peter and St Clare's Church are possibly a legacy from the Civil War.
Avon Dassett – St John the Baptist Church was rebuilt in 1868.
All Saints' Church – Known as the Cathedral of the Hills, this 13th-century church has an airy feel to its white interior. The floor slopes steeply uphill at the chancel end. Although once prosperous in the 13th century, the Black Death decimated Burton Dassett's population and the village died out in the 15th century when Sir Edward Belknap enclosed 600 acres evicting the tenants.

REFRESHMENTS:
The Merrie Lion, Fenny Compton.
Prince Rupert Inn, Avon Dassett.
There are also numerous picnic areas in the Country Park.

Walk 51 CHARLECOTE PARK AND HAMPTON LUCY 6m (9½km)
Maps: OS Sheets Landranger 151; Pathfinder 998.
An undulating walk via two interesting villages and a National
Trust house. Good views.
Start: At 264564, Charlecote Park car park.

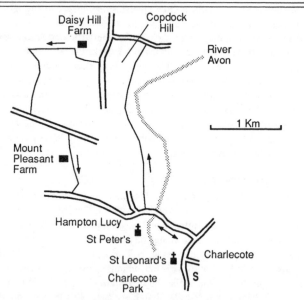

Turn right past St Leonard's Church and go along the boundary of Charlecote Park, where deer can usually be seen. Turn left down the minor road to **Hampton Lucy**. After crossing the bridge over the River Avon, turn right, down a track, then left across a meadow. Go over two stiles and walk inside a fence. Go through a gate and keep to the higher path when the way divides. Go through another gate and along a good headland at the edge of a wood. Return to the wood through a gate and re-emerge alongside a field, with good views left towards the Welcombe Hills Obelisk (*see* **Note** to Walk 22). Now keep the hedge on your right to the end of the field, then go through a gap in the corner. Keep straight ahead, past a line of oaks, all that remain of an old hedgerow. There are good views to Warwick Castle and St Mary's Church on the right. The path dips through a hedge, then skirts Copdock Hill, on the right, to reach a road – be careful on this last stretch as the path can be slippery. Go left, along the road, ignore side roads, until just before the top of the slope. There, turn right along an unmarked driveway to Daisy Hill Farm.

About 100 yards before the house, take the well-marked route over two stiles on the left. Turn right, and, at the edge of the farmyard, go over another stile and turn left. Now keep the hedge on your left, descending the pasture to cross another stile. Climb the slope ahead until the hedge turns sharply left: turn left with it and follow the signed bridleway to a minor road. Turn left along the road for $^1/_2$ mile, then turn right down a driveway, past a yellow arrow, to reach Mount Pleasant Farm. The path goes to the left of the farm buildings, past a telegraph pole, and then traverses a field beside the hedge on the left. Go through a gap in the hedge to reach a stile. The path here has been diverted to the right and follows the edge of the field to a road. Turn left and walk into Hampton Lucy. Go past the church and inn, turn right at a road junction and recross the bridge used earlier. Now follow the road back to **Charlecote Park.**

POINTS OF INTEREST:

Charlecote Park – The Park is open from April to October. Since 1247 it has been owned by the Lucy family and was given to the National Trust in 1946. The present house was built in 1558 by Sir Thomas Lucy and the deer park was landscaped by Capability Brown. Folklore has it that, as a young boy, Shakespeare was caught poaching deer in the park and was brought before the local magistrate, Sir Thomas Lucy, on whom he later based his character, Justice Shallow. St Leonard's Church was built in 1850 on the site of a smaller, 12th-century, church. Inside there are fine tombs of the Lucy family.

Hampton Lucy – A charming village remains despite much modern development. St Peter's Church dates from the 19th century, being built, at the expense of Reverend John Lucy, after the demolition of the medieval church in 1826. The east end was remodelled by Sir Gilbert Scott in 1858. To the north of the village is Hampton Wood which is in the care of Warwickshire Wildlife Trust and has an open day each Spring for the magnificent display of bluebells.

REFRESHMENTS:

The Boar's Head Inn, Hampton Lucy.
There are tea rooms at Charlecote Park.

Walk 52 **PRIORS MARSTON AND PRIORS HARDWICK** 6m (9^1/$_2$km)
Maps: OS Sheets Landranger 151; Pathfinder 999.
An enjoyable circuit, visiting two lovely churches and a canal.
Start: At 472562, the centre of Priors Hardwick.

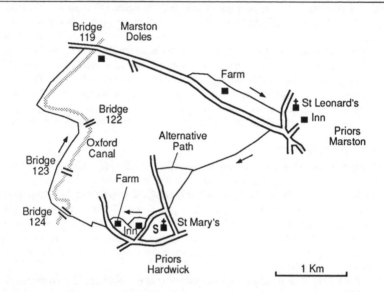

Walk past the village inn towards the church, turning immediately left down a driveway
marked with a yellow arrow. Go past houses on to an enclosed path between conifers,
following it into pasture. Head to the right of the buildings, and go through a gateway
to turn left past a farm. Turn left at a lane, go through a gate and immediately turn
right through another gate into a field. Keep the hedge on your right and aim for the
canal bridge. According to the OS map, the path goes through the right-hand gateway
ahead and along the field to the canal bridge (No. 124), although there are no arrows
to indicate the correct route. On reaching the bridge, turn right (north) up the towpath
of the Oxford Canal (*see* Note to Walk 8). The towpath has a well drained, firm surface
which is a delight to follow. At the third bridge, No. 119 (Nos. 121 and 120 have
vanished!) by Napton Top Lock at **Marston Doles**, leave the canal, turning right along
the road for almost a mile. The skyline ahead is dominated by a radio relay tower. Go

through a gateway on the left marked with a yellow arrow, and walk half-right through the hedgerow. Cross the next field to a marker post and go past the left side of some farm buildings. The path is well waymarked over the next fields: keep the hedge on the right. Climb over two stiles to emerge into **Priors Marston** opposite School Lane.

Turn right along the road to reach the green and war memorial. Turn right along the road to Southam, then go over a stile on the left and keep alongside the hedge on the left. Go through a gateway and uphill across pasture. Walk with the hedge on your left across a long field to reach a stile. Go over to join a horse trail (marked by white arrows). The line of this path has been diverted as the path on the ground does not match the line indicated by the OS map. On nearing the end of the field, watch for a path across the centre of the arable field on the left. This path is not always clearly marked or obvious underfoot, but aims for the hedge opposite to emerge by houses. Turn right and immediately left down a road to reach the church to **Priors Hardwick**. However, if the designated path is inaccessible, follow the path you are on to reach a gate and a road. Now turn left to reach a road junction: the village lies to the right.

POINTS OF INTEREST:
Marston Doles – This tiny hamlet, lies at the point where the Oxford Canal crosses the old Welsh road, used by drovers to move sheep from Wales to the London markets.
Priors Marston – The land here and at Priors Hardwick originally belonged to the Priors of Coventry, passing, after the Dissolution, to the Spencer family. St Leonard's Church, on the site of an earlier 13th-century building, was extensively rebuilt in 1863 and has a collection of interesting tombstones. On the floor of the porch is a bronze plaque to Richard West, who died in 1691, and in the churchyard are two magnificent cedar trees dating from the early 1800s.
Priors Hardwick – A thriving medieval village, depopulated firstly by plague and then the sheep enclosures. St Mary's Church dates from the late 13th century, although the nave was mostly rebuilt in the 1860s. Fragments of a slab mark the grave of a 15th-century knight. The modern lychgate was erected in 1862 to celebrate Queen Victoria's Jubilee.

REFRESHMENTS:
The Butcher's Arms, Priors Hardwick.
The Falcon Inn, Priors Marston.

Walk 53   **STONELEIGH AND BAGINTON**   6m (9^1/$_2$km)

Maps: OS Sheets Landranger 140; Pathfinder 955.

A walk along a riverside from a delightful village, visiting two
fascinating churches and a Roman fort.

Start: At 333727, the lay-by bridge on the B4113, Stoneleigh.

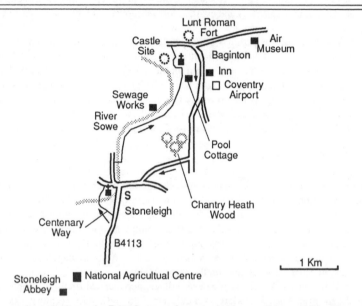

Turn southwards down the B4113, away from the bridge, walking uphill with good
views of **Stoneleigh**. Turn right through two gates to follow the Centenary Way (*see*
Note to Walk 34). Cross a field, aiming to the left of a pond, and swing right towards
a marker post. Beyond this an enclosed path is followed down Motslow Hill to a
bridge over the River Sowe. Go through the churchyard beyond, and turn left into
Church Lane. Turn right through the village and left up the B4113, with care, passing
a garage. After 300 yards, go through a gate on the right, by a small building, and
cross the River Sowe, over two bridges. Cross the meadow ahead, then turn left to
reach a stile. Go over and keep a hedge on your right to reach a stile. Cross and follow
the hedge (on your left this time) to a stile in the corner of the field. The waymarked
footpath now runs parallel to the river all the way to **Baginton**. Cross another field and

98

go around the boundary fence of a sewage works to reach a stile. Cross and turn left, then go right, along the bottom edge of the field. Maintain direction across fields and four stiles, and at the fifth, by a gate, cross a footbridge and go through a kissing gate near Pool Cottage.

Continue to reach a lane by Baginton Church. Go through the churchyard and a gate, and turn right. The tangled scrub on the left marks the site of Baginton Castle, but little remains and the area is on private land. Go alongside the churchyard hedge to reach a gate and then go left to reach a metal gate. Walk along the lane beyond to reach a road and turn right along Coventry Road, passing **Lunt Roman Fort**. Keep to Coventry Road, turning right with it. (From here the return route to Stoneleigh follows minor roads, as no footpaths cross nearby fields. The minor roads are normally fairly quiet, except at rush hour times when they are used as a 'rat run' by commuters. If young children or dogs are in the party, it might be easier to retrace the outward route by the river).

If returning by road, go past the Oak Inn and Coventry Airport (which houses the Midland Air Museum) and at the next fork turn right. After $^3/_4$ mile, turn right by Chantry Heath Wood, following a minor road to eventually reach a T-junction. Turn right down the hill to return to the start.

POINTS OF INTEREST:
Stoneleigh – A lovely village, with delightful half-timbered houses and a magnificent manor farmhouse. St Mary the Virgin's Church has box pews, a wooden gallery, a remarkable Norman chancel arch and a font with carvings of the Apostles. The pew cushions have beautiful tapestry designs, all sewn by volunteers. The almshouses were built in 1594 by Alice Leigh, the wife of Sir Thomas Leigh. Nearby Stoneleigh Abbey, whose 12th-century buildings were established by Cistercian monks, has been the home of the Leigh family since the 16th century. It now houses the National Agricultural Centre where the Royal Agricultural Show is held in July each year.
Baginton – St John the Baptist Church contains fine brasses of Sir William Bagot, one of the favourites of Richard II and the builder of the castle (which was excavated in the 1930s). In the churchyard are the graves of seven young Polish airmen whose aircraft crashed nearby in 1940.
Lunt Roman Fort – The fort dates from AD60. Some of the timber buildings were reconstructed by the Royal Engineers in 1971. In the grounds are the remains of a unique cavalry training ring.

REFRESHMENTS:
The Oak Inn, Baginton.

Walk 54   LAPWORTH AND PACKWOOD   6m (9¹/₂km)

Maps: OS Sheets Landranger 139; Pathfinder 954.

A National Trust house, a church and two canals add interest to this easy ramble.

Start: At 187709, the canal-side car park, Kingswood.

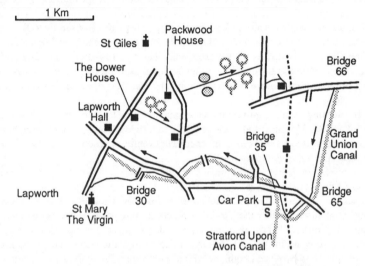

Walk left along the towpath of the Stratford-upon-Avon canal (*see* Note to Walk 68), go under Bridge 35, and past the Lapworth flight of locks to reach Bridge 30. Climb up the far side of the bridge, turn left through a handgate and walk along the cricket field fence to reach a stile in the corner. Do not go over the stile: instead, turn right, with a hedge on your right, to reach and cross another stile. Go straight ahead, descending to cross a stile by a pond. Go diagonally left across a lawn, along a well waymarked path, to reach a difficult stile. Cross the paddock beyond, go over a stile and follow the path ahead to St Mary the Virgin Church, **Lapworth.**

Turn right along a minor road, passing the War Memorial, erected in 1921. Go straight over the B4439, with care, into Grove Lane and, after passing Lapworth Hall and the Dower House, go over a stile on the right into the parkland of **Packwood House.**

100

Walk to the right of a group of pine trees and go over a stile into a field. Follow a headland around the left field edge and go over a stile. Climb past the side of a bungalow to reach a road. Turn left, and almost immediately left again at a junction to reach Packwood House.

Turn right through a gate opposite the House and walk along an avenue of horse chestnut trees. Go over a stile by ponds and continue to reach a minor road. Turn right, and after 200 yards go through a waymarked gate on the left into a field. Cross to reach a kissing gate. Go through, cross a drive and climb the fence opposite. Now skirt the edge of a garden and house to reach a drive. Walk down the drive and turn left along a road. Go over a railway bridge to reach the Grand Union Canal (*see* Note to Walk 5) at Bridge 66. Turn right along the towpath for a mile. Go under Bridge 65, and at the next bridge turn right along the small canal which links the Grand Union and Stratford-upon-Avon canals at Kingswood junction. Turn right along the towpath to return to the start.

POINTS OF INTEREST:

Lapworth – Although the original village developed around the church, after the construction of the canals and the railway in the 19th century, the nucleus of the village shifted, to centre on Kingswood. Alterations to St Mary the Virgin's Church around 1300 included adding a north aisle and the conversion of St James' Chapel into the south aisle. The chancel was restored in 1860, revealing the top of one of the original windows, but the roof was partly damaged by fire in 1876 and again in 1898. A small Runic cross in the churchyard is a memorial to four schoolchildren who drowned in nearby Spring Pit in 1907. One of the prime movers in the gunpowder plot, Robert Catesby, was born at Bushwood Hall, south of Lapworth, in 1573. He was a descendant of William Catesby, a loyal minister to Richard III.

Packwood House – A National Trust property and home of the Fetherston family until 1869. The house was bought in 1905 by Alfred Ash, who repaired and re-instated the 17th-century garden layout. The now famous topiary garden depicts the Sermon on the Mount. Cromwell's General, Henry Ireton, stayed here before the Battle of Edge Hill and another tradition claims Charles II halted here after the defeat at Worcester in 1651. Samuel Johnson's parents were married in nearby St Giles Church in 1706.

REFRESHMENTS:

The Boot Inn, Lapworth Flight.
The Navigation Inn, Kingswood Junction.

Walk 55　　　**WOOTTON WAWEN**　　　6m (9¹/₂km)

Maps: OS Sheets Landranger 151; Pathfinder 975.

An interesting canal walk past Wootton Wawen and through Austy Woods. Muddy in patches.

Start: At 162638, a pull-in on Pettiford Lane.

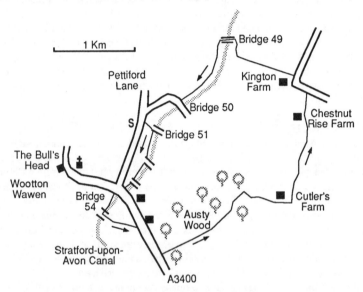

From the pull-in, where there is limited parking, take the bridleway eastwards to Bridge 51 and turn right along the towpath of the Stratford-upon-Avon Canal (*see* Note to Walk 68). Pass two bridges and cross the aqueduct over the A3400, from where access to **Wootton Wawen** is possible. Continue to the next bridge, No. 54, and go left through a gate. Turn left, and then right, with a copse of trees on the left, then walk across a field and go through the hedgerow in front. Go diagonally left and through the second metal gate. Turn right, with care, along the A3400, passing Austy Manor and a hotel sign nailed to a tree, then cross the road to reach a double metal gate. Go through and follow a bridleway into **Austy Wood**.

　　　Walk ahead, but after a short distance leave the wood, turning left and then swinging right along a field edge. Follow this boundary, with the wood on your left, past several small breaks in the wood until a larger break is reached. Here the path is signed half-left across grassland to re-enter Austy Wood. The path is well waymarked through the trees, climbing to join a bridleway at a T-junction. Turn right, through a gate, and go right again along the edge of a field. Turn left before the first hedgerow and descend towards Cutler's Farm. The bridleway is well marked through the farmyard to a farm track. Turn left and follow the lane for a mile, going over a stile and past Chestnut Rise Farm to emerge on to a lane by the farm entrance.

Turn right to reach a road junction, then left along a minor road. After the road swings right, passing Kington Farm, watch for a stile on the left. Go over and cross the field beyond to go over another stile. Turn immediately left and go through a gate ahead. Turn right, go through another gate and follow the track beyond, with a hedge on the left and a wire fence on the right. Go through a gate, then straight ahead across a field, passing through another hedgerow. Continue with a hedge on your right and, on reaching the canal, turn right over a stile and walk to bridge No. 49. Go over and turn left along the towpath to the next bridge, No. 50. Now turn right along the tarmac road to reach Pettiford Lane and the start.

POINTS OF INTEREST:

Wootton Wawen – A fascinating village which suffers from considerable through traffic. Wootton Hall, now part of a residential caravan park, is a late 17th-century mansion complete with ornamental weir and lake. It was the childhood home of Mrs Fitzherbert, whom the Prince of Wales, later George IV, secretly married in 1785, the marriage lasting until 1803. The late 18th-century mill was once powered by water from the River Alne. On the bridge parapet is a milestone, dated 1806, which shows an inaccurate one hundred miles to London. St Peter's Church has Saxon origins: the land was given to monks by Aethelbald, King of Mercia in the early 8th century. The fabric of the church has almost every style of medieval architecture from the 11th to the 17th centuries and many interesting monuments, in particular a 15th-century knight in alabaster, as well as early 16th-century brasses of John Harewell and family.
Austy Wood – A deciduous woodland with a healthy population of oak and ash and masses of field maple.

REFRESHMENTS:
The Bull's Head, Wootton Wawen.
The Navigation Inn, Wootton Wawen.

Walk 56   BADDESLEY CLINTON AND WROXALL   6m (9½km)

Maps: OS Sheets Landranger 139; Pathfinder 955.

A splendid walk through beautifully varied countryside. Muddy in patches.

Start: At 206707, the car park, Hay Wood.

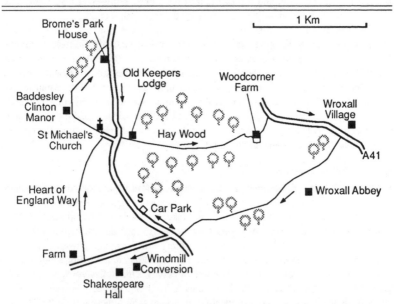

From the car park, turn left down the road. Go right at the first junction, passing an interesting windmill conversion and Shakespeare Hall on the left. Shortly, take the Heart of England Way (*see* Note to Walk 66) through a muddy gateway on the right. Follow the lane past a farm, but when it bends left, go ahead through a gate and along the hedge on the left. Go through a gate and over a footbridge, then aim for the top right corner of a field. The enclosed path beyond the gate leads to a lane by **Baddesley Clinton** Church. (A possible short cut goes right, along the lane to the entrance of Hay Wood). Turn left through the churchyard, passing the entrance to the manor and then going right past a car park.

Go along a drive for about 100 yards, then turn right, through a gate. The path beyond skirts a small wood and crosses stiles to reach a lane by Brome's Park House.

Here, leave the Heart of England Way, turning right down the lane. Go left down the lane past Old Keeper's Lodge – the lane behind is the short cut from the church – and enter **Hay Wood**. Follow a well-marked bridleway, crossing a forest road, to reach a gate on the far side. Go through into a field. Cross diagonally right, go through a gate and turn left to reach another gate. Go through and turn left along a drive. Turn right by Woodcorner Farm to reach the A41. Turn right, with care, along the road, passing the Wroxall village sign. Now watch for the estate road, on the right, signed to Quarry Lane. Go over a stile and follow the lane past a coppice, on the right. When the lane swings left towards the buildings of **Wroxall Abbey**, go through a metal gate on the right. Cross the field beyond, walking to the left of a large clump of trees and past a line of cedars. Aim for the gate in the bottom right corner of the field, climb a stile and walk straight ahead, following the line of a long removed hedgerow which is still marked by the occasional tree. Once over the rise, walk parallel to the copse on the right. Go over a stile in the top right corner, and walk beside the fence on the right to reach a gate on to a lane. Turn right along the road to return to the car park.

POINTS OF INTEREST:
Baddesley Clinton – The manor was bought by John Brome in 1438. In 1517 his granddaughter married into the Ferrers family who held the manor in an unbroken line until 1939. Now cared for by the National Trust, it is open from March to September. St Michael's Church was once called St James, possibly changing its dedication following restoration in the 19th century. In season, the churchyard is full of primroses, daffodils, violets and bluebells. Nicholas Brome, who inherited the manor in 1483, built the tower as atonement for killing a priest who he thought was having an affair with his wife. As a further penance, Nicholas was buried inside the south doorway so that anyone entering walks across his grave.
Hay Wood – Once part of the Baddesley Clinton estate, the 200 acres of woodland are now managed by the Forestry Commission. Although mostly planted with conifers, there are also oak, rowan, birch and holly, and the fairly open canopy encourages the growth of wild flowers. Considering the mass of conifers, it is difficult to imagine that this wood is a fragment of the ancient Forest of Arden.
Wroxall Abbey – The abbey was founded by Benedictine nuns in 1135, but only St Leonard's Church and part of the cloisters remain. An Elizabethan house, lived in by Christopher Wren, was demolished and the present Victorian mansion, now a school was built in 1864.

REFRESHMENTS:
There are tea rooms at Baddesley Clinton when the manor is open.

Walk 57   **BRAILES**   6m (9½km)

Maps: OS Sheets Landranger 151; Pathfinder 1044 and 1021.

A superb walk, with glorious views to three villages, an old castle site and a cathedral.

Start: At 305395, a lay-by just south of Upper Brailes.

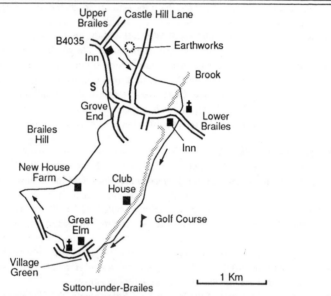

From the lay-by, head north up the B4035 through **Upper Brailes** and turn right up Castle Hill Lane. Take the path on the right, just before the last houses, and cross fields to the earthworks on Castle Hill, the remains of a 12th-century castle built by the Earl of Warwick. Skirt the earthworks on the right to reach a stile in the right-hand corner. Follow the path beyond across a field to a stile by a gate. Cross the stile opposite and cross a field to another stile by a gate. Cross to a further stile, following the enclosed path beyond down steps to a bridge. Turn half-right to a stile in front of the church. Turn right into **Lower Brailes**.

An alleyway before the inn leads to a path junction. Go over two stiles and keep a brook on your right across two fields. Follow the hedge on the right to a farm lane. Turn left over a cattle grid and then right through a metal gate. Follow a path along the right field edge, by a brook, to reach a stile by the golf course. (Despite the plea to keep to the footpath, there are few marker posts to help). Keep the brook on your right, go over a footbridge and along a gravel track, passing the clubhouse to reach a blue arrow and a path, half-left, to a stile. Turn right along a lane. Go over a stile on the left and head half-right to a footbridge. Now aim for a stile halfway up the fence on the left. Go over, cross two fields and turn right into **Sutton-under-Brailes.**

Turn left at the village green to reach the church. Go over the stile up the drive on the left, cross a pasture and go over another stile. Go half-left across a field to a lane. Turn right, go through a gate at the lane end and climb a field with a fence on your left. At the top, follow the hedge on the right to reach a clump of pine trees. Just past the trees, turn right through a gate to join a bridle-way skirting Brailes Hill. Keep a hedge on your right across two fields to New House Farm. Turn right, and then left, with the farm on your right, to where the track swings right. There, continue ahead through a gate. At the end of the field beyond, go through a gate on to a sheltered path between trees. Follow the path to a steep dingle, continuing along a muddy, slippery path, downhill. Go left over a stile halfway down and cross a field to its far right corner. Go over a stile and turn right, downhill, to reach a lane in Grove End. Turn left and, just past a power pole, go over a stile on the left. Head for the top right corner, cross another stile and then head straight across a field to Upper Brailes.

POINTS OF INTEREST:
Upper Brailes – The village was granted a charter in 1248 and developed into an important market centre, with a prosperous wool trade and a thriving water mill. The Catholic church of St Peter and St Paul, built in 1726, is in the upper storey of a barn.
Lower Brailes – The 14th-century St George's Church is known as the Cathedral of the Feldon and was extensively rebuilt in 1649 after possibly being damaged in the Civil War. It has a massive, 120 foot, 15th-century tower. Inside the door is a weathered effigy of a priest dating from 1450. The model of the church took 7 years to complete using 250,000 matchsticks. In the churchyard is an unusual grave to the Sheldon family, adorned with Egyptian columns.
Sutton-under-Brailes – The church of St Thomas à Becket has a Norman nave and a 13th-century chancel. On the village green is a Victorian postbox and a tree stump of the Great Elm of Sutton, which reached 150 feet before falling down in 1967.

REFRESHMENTS:
The Gate Inn, Upper Brailes.
The George Hotel, Lower Brailes.

Walk 58   **FRANKLEY AND BARTLEY RESERVOIR**   6m (9$^1/_2$km)
Maps: OS Sheets Landranger 139; Pathfinder 933 and 953.
*An enjoyable walk in surprisingly rural countryside, either side
of the motorway.*
Start: At 999812, Scotland Lane, west side of Bartley reservoir.

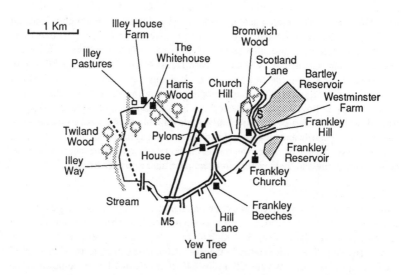

With **Bartley reservoir** on your left, walk down Scotland Lane and turn right up
Frankley hill. From the church, take the hedged track heading south-westwards, going
under pylon lines and over a stile. Follow a field edge uphill to emerge opposite
Frankley Beeches. Cross the stile to the right of the trees and walk down to Hill Lane.
Turn left, then shortly right along Yew Tree Lane. Cross the M5, then climb a stile on
the right. Follow the right hedge round to a stile by a water tank, then keep a hedge on
your left through two fields and a gateway. Turn left, then, shortly, right across a field
to a stile. Cross the stile opposite and another ahead to cross the disused railway into
a field. Aim for the protruding fence corner ahead, then for the top left corner. There,
turn right along the green lane, joining the Illey Way, a waymarked path linking
Woodgate and Waseley Country Parks.

Keep the fence on your right at first, switching sides halfway to reach a stile into Twiland Wood. Follow the stony path through the wood, then go down steps, passing the site of the Dowry Dell viaduct. Built in 1881, it carried the Old Hill to Longbridge railway and was 600 feet long and 100 feet high: it was dismantled in 1965, the only visible remains being the blue brick bases. Climb steps and cross the centre of a field to a stile and four-way signpost. Turn right, still on the Illey Way, and cross a stile and footbridge. Turn left over another footbridge into **Illey Pastures**. Here, please walk in single file and do not trample or pick the wildflowers.

At the end of the second field, go over a stile by a gate, walk past Illey House farm and along the lane ahead. Turn right up the drive of The Whitehouse and join a green lane to the left of the garage. Cross a stream and, shortly, climb a stile on the left. Walk through Harris Wood and cross a stile into a field. Follow the left hedge to the top right corner and turn left, with a hedge on your right. Cross two fields and go under the M5. Turn right along a lane, then go left under pylon lines, and along a field edge. At a marker post, go left through Raven Hays Wood, then head for the top left corner of the field to reach Frankley Green. Turn left. Go straight over at a crossroads, going down Church Hill and under pylon lines to reach a stile on the left. Go over and straight across two fields, passing to the left of Westminster Farm, to the edge of an estate. Turn right to reach Bromwich Wood. Numerous paths lead through this bluebell wood back to the reservoir.

POINTS OF INTEREST:
Bartley Reservoir – A church, chapel and school were demolished to make way for the reservoir which was completed in 1930.
Frankley – Frankley Manor was destroyed in the Civil War, the stone later being used in the nave of St Leonard's Church. The remains of an Anglo Saxon cross shaft can be seen in the churchyard. The tower, which is also of stone taken from Frankley Manor, was added to the 12th-century nave in 1751. The clump of Frankley Beeches, standing at 829 feet on top of Egg Hill, is a familiar landmark. It is believed they were planted by an ancestor of Lord Cobham to commemorate the Great Exhibition in 1851. The Cadbury family bought the land and presented it to the National Trust in 1932 to mark their company's jubilee.
Illey Pastures – These two ancient meadows, untainted by either chemicals or the plough, support a variety of rare plants including common spotted orchid, sneezewort and pepper saxifrage.

REFRESHMENTS:
None on the route. The nearest is *The Black Horse* in Illey.

Walk 59 THE BRATCH AND ORTON 6m (9½km)

Maps: OS Sheets Landranger 139; Pathfinder 912.

A splendid walk along a dismantled railway and canal on the outskirts of the area.

Start: At 867938, the picnic site car park, Bratch Locks.

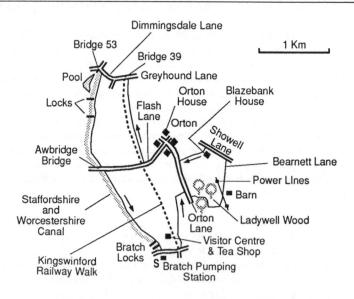

From the car park, turn right along the road, passing the Pumping Station and going under a railway bridge. Turn left to the Kingswinford Railway Walk (*see* Note to Walk 72) Visitor Centre (where there is alternative parking). At the end of the car park, turn right up steps and then go left through a kissing gate. Follow a path along the rear of gardens to the end of the field. Turn right, beside a fence, and go through a paddock to reach Orton Lane. Cross and turn right along the pavement. Just past the second house, go left up an alleyway on to a path which climbs through Ladywell Wood. As you emerge from the trees, go ahead up steps, then veer right through trees to reach a field. Go straight across, towards the pylon lines, then turn left along Bearnett Lane, with wonderful open views to the Welsh hills.

Go past a barn, continuing to reach Showell Lane. Turn left, dropping steeply downhill. Just past Blazebank House, go over a stile on the left and follow the footpath beyond, skirting the edge of a garden. Go over a stile and descend a steep bank to another. Go over and keep a wood on your right until you are just past a water trough, then veer slightly left to reach a stile by a gate in front of buildings. Turn right along Orton Lane and at the crossroads in **Orton**, turn left down Flash Lane to reach Bridge No. 36 on the Kingswinford Railway Walk. Turn right up the dismantled railway to the Greyhound Lane bridge (No. 39). There, leave the railway via the steps on the far side.

Turn right up the road. Ignore a left turn to Wombourne, going down Dimmingsdale Lane to reach Dimmingsdale Bridge (No. 53) on the **Staffordshire and Worcestershire Canal**. Turn left down the newly improved towpath for two miles, passing Awbridge lock and bridge to reach **The Bratch** bridge (No. 47) and locks. The car park is on the other side of the road.

POINTS OF INTEREST:

Orton – The village was known as Overton until the late 16th century. The 18th-century Orton House has an insurance plate by a window which would have been essential to the Insurance Company's Fire Brigade. No plate and they would not have put out a fire!

Staffordshire and Worcestershire Canal – The canal was built by James Brindley to link the Midlands with the River Severn and opened in 1722. It runs for 46 miles, from Great Haywood to Stourport, and passes through lovely, unspoilt countryside. The circular side weirs are unique to this canal and occupy less space than a conventional weir of equal capacity. Awbridge Lock is crossed by the only original bridge remaining on the canal, and is believed to be Brindley's first attempt at building a canal bridge and a lock on a public road. The bridge parapet is unusual, having nine brick pillars.

The Bratch – This set of three locks, opened in 1772, is where the canal drops 30 feet into the Smestow valley. The striking octagonal building with a central chimney is thought to be the old toll house. Bratch Pumping Station, an amazing building resembling a French chateau with four corner turrets and decorative red, buff and blue bricks, was opened in 1897 to supply the Wombourne and Bilston areas. Since 1960 it has been powered by electricity but the original steam engines have been preserved.

REFRESHMENTS:

Ye Olde Station Tea Shoppe at the Visitor Centre, Kingswinford Railway.

Walk 60   WASELEY AND BEACON HILL   6m (9½km)

Maps: OS Sheets Landranger 139; Pathfinder 953.

A terrific walk over two country parks. Spectacular views and excellent footpaths.

Start: At 972783, the Visitor Centre, Waseley Country Park.

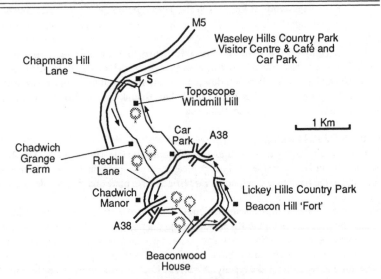

Go through the gate (with several signposts) to the left of the Centre to reach open grassland. Turn right along a fence to join the North Worcestershire Path (*see* Note to Walk 64). Walk ahead to reach Chapmans Hill Lane. Turn left, then veer left at a junction by a sign to 'The Cottage'. Walk past a farm (where the N. W. Path goes right), swinging left on to a muddy track. On reaching the gap ahead, bear left along a path which soon narrows. Ignore a stile on the right and cross a brook to reach two stiles. Ignore the stile on the left, going ahead to reach the Chadwich estate. Keep a hedge on your right, go through a gate and past a cottage. Cross a drive and follow the path ahead. On nearing Chadwich Grange Farm, over to the right, climb the stile ahead and cross the centre of the field beyond, aiming towards the left corner of the wood on the right. Just before the wood, cross a stile on the right. Walk through the wood and along a drive to reach Redhill Lane. Turn right.

Go past Chadwich Manor, then under the A38 to reach a T-junction. Turn left and, shortly, right along a bridleway. Walk up a drive between houses to reach a gate into the wood. Head steeply uphill to reach a lane by a farm. Turn left. Opposite the drive to Beaconwood House, go through a gate on the right, by a National Trust sign, and head diagonally left across two fields. Cross a drive and the field beyond to reach a lane. Turn left to reach the Beacon Hill car park in the **Lickey Hills Country Park**. Go through the car park to the 'Fort' viewpoint, then turn left along the escarpment. Skirt in front of the trees, then turn right before a stile and drop downhill. Now keep parallel to a lane on the left to reach a road. Turn left and just past a dangerous left bend, turn right down a bridleway to rejoin the North Worcestershire Path. Follow the Path to a road.

Turn left, go over the A38 and turn left again into Holywell Lane. Shortly, turn right into the south car park of the **Waseley Hills Country Park**. Keep left through the car park, go right past a noticeboard and through a gate (still following the N. W. Path). Head uphill towards a bench, then veer right along the high ground, Go through two gates and climb Waseley Hill. Go past a marker post and a plantation and head for the toposcope on Windmill Hill. Downhill and under the line of pylons is the car park.

POINTS OF INTEREST:
Lickey Hills Country Park – Beacon Hill was once part of the early warning beacon system and is now crowned with a 'modern' stone fort and a toposcope. A stone fountain commemorates the gift of this land in 1907 by the Cadbury family.
Waseley Hills Country Park – The Park's 150 acres stand on the fringe of Birmingham and are extremely popular with Midlands residents, welcoming over 200,000 visitors every year. The open grassland, scattered pockets of gorse and woodland are a joy to explore. Windmill Hill, at 1,013 feet, offers views ranging from the Birmingham connurbation to the hills of Wales and Worcestershire. The Park's hills are a natural watershed, with rainfall draining east to the Trent valley and the North Sea and west to the Bristol Channel via the River Salwarpe. The park belonged to nearby Chadwich Manor until the 16th century. Following the Dissolution, the land was given to Christchurch, and in 1904 was bought by the Cadbury family, who donated the hills to the National Trust.

REFRESHMENTS:
There is a cafe at the Waseley Country Park Visitor Centre.

Walk 61   **BRINKLOW AND EASENHALL**   6m (9$\frac{1}{2}$km)
Maps: OS Sheets Landranger 140; Pathfinder 956 and 936.
*A walk from the site of an ancient castle, along a canal and over
farmland. Some muddy paths.*
Start: At 435793, Broad Street, Brinklow.

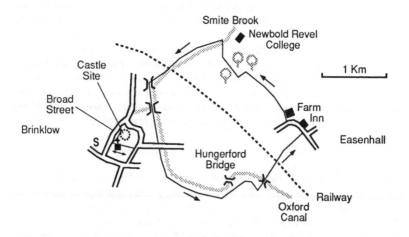

Walk north up Broad Street (the B4027) and turn right down an alleyway between the
Raven Inn and a garage. Cross a stile and go up the steps into the castle earthworks.
Bear left along the main path skirting the earthworks, although few will be able to
resist the scramble to the top to enjoy the lovely views. Go over a stile on to a lane and
turn right down it to a T-junction. The stile on the right is crossed on the return route.
Turn left to a bridge over the Oxford Canal (*see* Note to Walk 8). Turn right along the
towpath, going under Hungerford bridge (No. 35).

At the next bridge, leave the canal, crossing the bridge and heading straight
across the field. Go over a railway footbridge and up the field beyond. Go through a
gate in the middle of the far hedge and turn half-right to reach a stile. Go up the
alleyway into **Easenhall**. Turn left, past the inn, and, at a left bend, turn right up a

farm lane signed 'Bridle road to Stretton under Fosse'. Walk through the farm buildings, go through a gate on the left and turn immediately right to another gate. Keep the fence on your left to another gate. There is no path in the field beyond, so follow the vehicle tracks, keeping the hedge on your right, to join a wider track at the end, near trees.

Turn left along the track, passing the trees, then swing right to eventually enter the woods. Keep on the main track to emerge by the end of the lake and the grounds of **Newbold Revel**. A footpath joins from the left: the track bears left at the next gate to reach a bridleway. On reaching a tarmac drive, turn immediately left into the field – there is a marker on a tree. Follow a narrow path through the field, with Smite Brook on the left. Keep the brook on the left across further fields, go under the railway and along the next field edge to follow the path *under* the canal bridge. Turn right up a slippery path on the far side, and turn right along the canal towpath. Cross a bridge over a disused arm of the canal, then, at the next bridge, leave the canal, turning left along the road used on the outward route to reach the road junction. Cross the stile ahead and follow a path across two fields, with the earthworks to your right. In the top right corner of the second field, go down the alleyway into **Brinklow**.

POINTS OF INTEREST:

Easenhall – The village inn dates from 1640 and still has the original wattle and daub wall. The brick chapel, now converted into a house, dates back to 1873.

Newbold Revel Estate – Sir Thomas Mallory, author of *Morte d'Arthur*, inherited the house in 1433. The old house was replaced in 1716 with a modern building, later refurbished as a training college.

Brinklow – The village stands on the line of the Roman Fosse Way. It was granted a weekly market and fair in the 14th century and by 1646 had seven alehouses. Only earthworks remain of the Norman motte and bailey castle, known locally as The Tump, which was probably built around 1140 by the Earl of Leicester. The 13th-century St John the Baptist Church was built by the monks of Kenilworth and partly rebuilt in the 15th century. The interior was substantially altered in the 19th century. There is a difference in height of 12 feet from the west to east ends of the church. Fragments of old glass in roundels depict birds and a window shows the Last Judgement. In the churchyard is an interesting gravestone to Thomas Bolton, a deaf and dumb woodcarver who died in 1779, with the tools of his trade etched on his gravestone.

REFRESHMENTS:
The Golden Lion, Easenhall.
There are also several possibilities in Brinklow.

Walk 62   LEAMINGTON HASTINGS   6m (9½km)

Maps: OS Sheets Landranger 151; Pathfinder 977.

Pleasant open countryside and a delightful stretch of canal make up this easy walk.

Start: At 438653, the Birdingbury canal bridge on the A426.

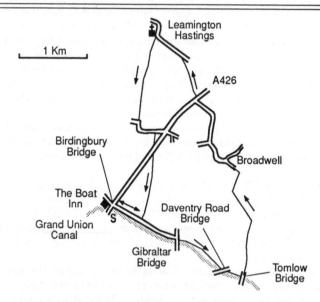

Parking is possible near the canal bridge.

From the bridge, walk left (south-eastwards) along the towpath of the Grand Union Canal (*see* Note to Walk 5). Go under Gibraltar Bridge and Daventry Road Bridge. Leave the canal at the third bridge, Tomlow Bridge, going left on to a lane and then through the gate opposite the bridge into a field. Follow the hedge on the right, passing through another gate and then veering half-left to go through a third gate in the middle of the far hedge. Bear left to reach the hedge on the left and head for the top left corner of the field, by the remains of a barn, now a horse jump. Turn left along the field edge (keeping the hedge on your right) and, after 200 yards, turn right over another jump. Head diagonally left over the field to its top left corner and go through a gap in the hedge. Continue diagonally left to join a track. Turn right towards a farm. Bear left alongside a fence, then go through a gate on the right. Cross to the gate ahead, go through and turn left along a lane which leads into Broadwell.

Walk ahead through the village, following the road as it curves right, passing a chapel. Now just by a left bend, level with the barns, turn right down a gated lane, following it as it eventually veers left to reach the A426. Cross, with care, and go over the stile opposite. Walk ahead to meet the hedge on the right, then aim for the top right corner. Go over the left-hand stile and follow the hedge on the right to reach a stile in the top right corner. Go over and follow the hedge on the right through two fields to reach a lane in **Leamington Hastings.**

Turn left into the village and, at a right bend, go left along a track. After $^1/_4$ mile, go past a barn (to the right) and through a gate. After a further 100 yards, you will come to a fork in the path: go through the gate and turn left to follow the hedge on the left. Follow the hedge through three fields to reach a minor road. Walk ahead, then go left with the road, but after 250 yards, by a power pole, go over a stile on the right. Follow the hedge on the left across the field to reach the A426. Recross this busy road with care, go over a stile by the gate opposite and follow the hedge on the right over several fields to reach a lane. Turn right up the towpath of the canal to return to the start.

POINTS OF INTEREST:
Leamington Hastings – The name derives from the Hastang family who held the manor in the 13th century. The Almshouses were recently restored but originally date from 1696. All Saints Church was built mostly in the 13th century. The west window has heraldic designs, the Early English nave has a boarded ceiling and late Gothic revival woodwork serves as a chancel arch. The chancel itself has 17th-century windows and a moulded cornice. There is also a bust of Sir Thomas Trevor, one of Charles I's Barons of the Exchequer. In the churchyard there are magnificent spreading yew trees.

REFRESHMENTS:
The Boat Inn, on the canal, just off A426 by the start of walk.

Walk 63 WINDMILL END AND NETHERTON TUNNEL 6m (9½km)
Maps: OS Sheets Landranger 139; Pathfinder 933 and 912.
A partly subterranean walk, deep in the Black Country. Torch essential!
Start: At 954882, the car park at Windmill End.

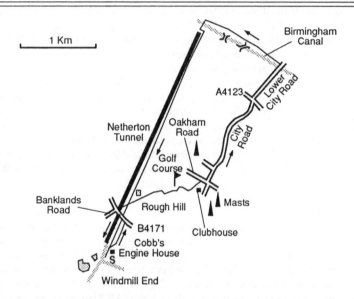

From the car park, climb up to the towpath, then turn right for a short distance to ascend to Cobbs Engine House. Continue past the Engine House into Warrens Hall Park. Head uphill through the Park and turn left along the B4171. Almost opposite Banklands Road, turn right along a footpath which climbs Rough Hill. Follow the fence and hedge on the left, passing a pool. At the top of the rise you will reach a gate. The main track swings left, but you turn right over two stiles to emerge on to a tarmac quarry road. Turn left along the road and, at a sharp left bend, go over a stile on the right on to a golf course. The path across the course is not well marked, so aim for the two masts at the top of Turners Hill and, on nearing the Clubhouse, turn left heading to the left of a hedge and fence: the two masts are now to your right and the single Darby Hill mast is to your left. Follow the path to reach Oakham Road by a bus stop.

There is now some necessary road walking to reach the tunnel entrance. Turn right, past the inn, and left down City Road for over a mile, crossing the A4123, with care, and heading down Lower City Road to reach the Birmingham Canal at Brades village. Join the towpath and head north-westwards, with the canal on your left. Go under two bridges to reach the **Netherton Tunnel** branch canal. Cross the bridge and turn right behind the house. Go down the slope then right along the towpath a short distance before entering Netherton Tunnel.

Most of the route so far could be tackled in trainers but waterproof boots are more suitable for the tunnel path, which is invariably muddy and wet. Although children will find walking through the tunnel in the dark exciting, this is no place for fooling about and both they and dogs should be kept under control. Needless to say a torch is essential as there is almost two miles of tunnel walking before you emerge into daylight at the south portal. Continue along the towpath to reach the **Windmill End Junction** and the start.

POINTS OF INTEREST:
Netherton Tunnel – Originally opened in 1858, this was the last working canal tunnel to be built in Britain. It is 3,027 yards long and 453 feet above sea level. It is 17 feet wide at the water level and has twin towpaths. The tunnel passes through the limestone rock and in some places where water has seeped through, stalactite columns and curtains have formed and can be seen hanging from the roof.
Windmill End Junction – This is where the Netherton Tunnel Approach Canal and the Dudley No. 2 Canal meet. The four cast iron footbridges were built by the Toll End Iron Works and the bridge nearest the tunnel entrance is now a Grade II listed structure. The Cobbs Engine House once housed a Watt beam engine which was used to pump water from the deep coal mines in the area into the canal. Built in 1831, it continued working until 1928. The huge chimney, 95 feet high, is a prominent landmark for miles around.

REFRESHMENTS:
The Dry Dock, Windmill End.
The Huntsman, on the A4123.
The Wheatsheaf, Oakham Road.

Walk 64 **LICKEY HILLS AND BITTELL RESERVOIRS** $6\frac{1}{2}$m ($10\frac{1}{2}$km)
Maps: OS Sheets Landranger 139; Pathfinder 953 and 954.
Beautiful wooded hills, two reservoirs and a canal add interest
to an excellent walk.
Start: At 998755, the Visitor Centre car park, Lickey Hills.

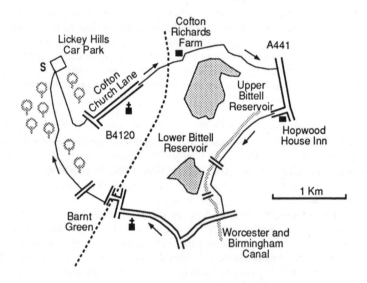

At the end of **Lickey Hills** car park, take the right forking path, through conifers, ignoring all side tracks. After passing a superb vantage point, the path loses height and swings left. Then, in sight of a road, it turns right downhill. By a bridleway sign, cross the road, turning right and almost immediately left into Cofton Church Lane. The road enters open countryside and passes St Michael's Church. Walk under the railway bridge and continue up a private drive towards Cofton Richards Farm. At this point the route joins the **North Worcestershire Path** and is well waymarked. Before reaching the farm, turn right through a gate, and then go left, past another waymark arrow, into a field. Upper Bittell Reservoir now appears on the right: at the next arrow, walk across the centre of a field towards the reservoir and past another stile. Follow the right edge of the field to reach a stile and a footbridge. Follow the muddy path beyond between a hedge and a wire fence, and then go over a footbridge, the path running close to the water. Where the Worcestershire Path turns left, continue straight on, going over a stile into a meadow. At the far side, by a gate, cross a stile into a lane which leads to the busy A441 in Hopwood.

Turn right and walk along the pavement to reach the Hopwood House Inn, on the right. Go over a canal bridge, turning right to join the muddy towpath of the **Worcester and Birmingham Canal.** Go under a bridge (Number 66) and past boat moorings with the Lower Bittell Reservoir on your right. Go under another bridge (Number 65), soon reaching an aqueduct. Go down steps on the far side to a road. Turn left, uphill, and go over a railway bridge to reach a T-junction. Turn right and walk down a road, past houses and under a railway bridge. Go straight over at a crossroads to reach Barnt Green. Walk past St Andrew's Church and turn right at a T-junction. Turn left up Station Approach, cross the railway by steps and turn left. Now go right by a signpost, into a delightful, tree-lined avenue which climbs to reach a lane. Cross and follow the bridleway opposite.

Follow the way through mixed woodland, keeping right of a shelter, and ignoring all side tracks. Go past several seats and then drop downhill, crossing a footbridge. Ignore a right turn and walk past another shelter. Keep straight on as a path joins from the right, then, when the main path goes left, keep right past a picnic area and sculpture, and climb gradually by trees to arrive back at the visitor centre.

POINTS OF INTEREST:

Lickey Hills – Designated a Country Park in 1971, its 524 acres of deciduous woodland and open heathland offer a wide range of habitats. The trees include plantations of Scots Pine, Douglas Fir, Norway Spruce and Larch. Other trees to be found are Oak, Hazel, Rowan, Beech, Birch and Holly: these provide food and shelter for a variety of wildlife. Birds include Fieldfares, Woodpeckers, Treecreepers and Nuthatches. The Beacon, at 975 feet (297m), is one of several viewpoints, with up to twelve counties visible on a clear day. A Monument was erected by the Worcestershire Regiment of Yeomanry Cavalry in 1834 to honour their founder, the sixth Earl of Plymouth.

North Worcestershire Path – The Path stretches for 26 miles from Kingsford Country Park to Forhill on the Roman Icknield Street.

Worcester and Birmingham Canal – The canal runs for 30 miles from Gas Street Basin in Birmingham to Worcester, with 58 locks and 5 tunnels.

REFRESHMENTS:

Hopwood House Inn, Hopwood.

There is also a cafe at Visitor Centre and plenty of picnic sites.

Walk 65   **SUTTON PARK**   6¹/₂m (10¹/₂km)

Maps: OS Sheets Landranger 139; Pathfinder 913.

*Wonderful open parkland, woods, pools and heathland in the
heart of Birmingham. Excellent footpaths.*

Start: At 114963, the Visitor Centre, Town Gate, Sutton Park.

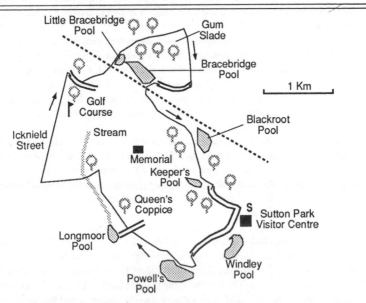

Walk past the **Sutton Park** Visitor Centre, on the left, and along the grass road verge.
Ignore a left turn by Wyndley Pool, continuing to a T-junction. Turn left towards
Powell's Pool. Just before the playground, turn right and walk across open grass,
between trees and the pool. Where the path swings left, look for a narrow opening on
the right through a belt of trees. Take this, emerging by heathland. Turn left and walk
past the golf course fence and through heathland to reach a road. On the left is
Longmoor Pool, but the path crosses straight over, passing to the left of a circle of
trees, the Queen's Coppice – planted in 1953 to commemorate Queen Elizabeth's
Coronation. Follow the footpath across Rowton Heath towards a low ridge. After a
path joins from the left, you reach a junction of tracks: turn left, and on joining a wide
track, which crosses a brook, turn left again, past another copse and an expanse of

heather. Now, turn right at the first crossroads. The path slants across the open heath to join the Roman road of Icknield Street and then crosses a golf course. After $1/_2$ mile, ford a shallow brook, bear right over another fairway and go through an oak glade. Turn right along a road to reach a car park. Turn left, and at the end of the car park, go through a gate on to a railway bridge. Turn left over the bridge: the path soon curves right to emerge by Little Bracebridge Pool.

Go past the pool, then ignore the first fork in the path but, at the second fork, a few yards further on, bear right. Another path joins from the left: continue to reach a crossroads. Turn left past Silver Birches, and at the next crossroads, by a bench, go straight ahead, along the edge of woodland. At the next junction of tracks, turn half-left – not fully left as that path turns back on itself. The TV transmitter seen ahead should indicate the route, if the leaves are not obscuring the view! At a T-junction, turn right and almost immediately right again on to a narrow path in a grassy clearing. Follow the path as it winds through the enchanting Gum Slade Wood. Turn right at the park road and right again at the next road junction, walking uphill through a car park to reach Bracebridge Pool. Walk along the left side of the pool and at the end re-cross the railway. Turn left along a well-defined track through woodland, ignoring all side turns. Go through a gate and bear right through another gate (with a redundant stile). On reaching Blackroot Pool, keep along the edge of the pool into woodland. Follow the path to Keeper's Pool, at the end of which turn left, through a gate, and follow the park road back to the Visitor Centre.

POINTS OF INTEREST:

Sutton Park – The Park's 2500 acres, now an SSSI, are a remnant of the heath and forest which once covered much of the Midlands. Encircled by roads, crossed by a railway, and with the centre of Birmingham nearby, it is an oasis of deciduous woodland, lowland heath and wetlands. Over 400 different flowers flourish here and the woods contain Oak, Holly, Rowan and Beech. There are many rare plants in the pools and bird life abounds. It was once a Royal Forest and hunting ground, and in 1100 passed to the Earl of Warwick and then Sir Ralph Bracebridge, who obtained the lease on the manor and chase from the Earl in 1419. After the Wars of the Roses, the lands were forfeited to the King. In the 16th century, Henry VIII presented the lands of Sutton Chase to Vesey, Bishop of Exeter and a native of Sutton Coldfield, who gave them to the people of the town in perpetuity. The railway was built across the park in the late 19th century.

REFRESHMENTS:

There are cafes and kiosks at the various park entrances.

Walk 66   **HENLEY-IN-ARDEN**   6$\frac{1}{2}$m (10$\frac{1}{2}$km)

Maps: OS Sheets Landranger 151 and 150; Pathfinder 975.

Pleasant rural walk from a historical town, across fields and skirting woodland.

Start: At 153657, Prince Harry Road car park, Henley-in-Arden.

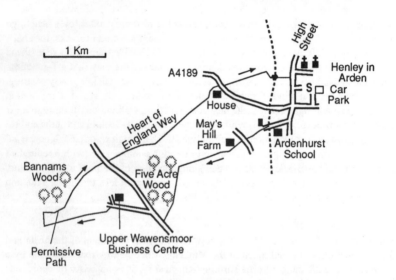

From the car park follow signs to the High Street, and turn left, past the famous Ice Cream factory. Go straight across the traffic lights and take the first lane on the right, signed to Ardenhurst School. At its end, go through a gate to the left of a house and then over a stile to the right of a brick barn. Walk across pasture, go over another stile and head downhill, alongside an old hedge, to reach a minor road. Cross and climb a stile. Cross the field beyond, with May's Hill Farm on your right. Go through two gates, and walk, with a fence on the left, to a gated track by a pond. Follow the track past a barn to reach a stile by a metal gate. Walk across a long meadow to the top left corner, go over a stile and continue to another stile into a field with Five Acre Wood on the right. Cross diagonally to the hedge on the left to reach a gate and stile in the top left corner. Walk straight across the next field to reach a minor road.

Turn right, then take the first left turn leading to Upper Wawensmoor Business Centre. Just before the old farmhouse, take the bridleway on the left, down a lane. Ignore a footpath straight ahead and turn right, still on the bridleway. When the track ends, continue across fields to reach a gate. Do not go through: instead, turn right up the slope. You are now following the **Heart of England Way**, and will do so all the way to **Henley-in-Arden**. Keep close to Bannams Wood, on the left, on a permissive path through a gate and over two stiles. A public footpath from the woods joins from the left, and the path drops downhill to a road.

Cross and walk along the hedge through two fields. Climb the slope and pass a gateway, on the left, and a metal tank. Now go over the stile on the left and cross diagonally to reach another stile. Go over and drop downhill to a bridge in the far left corner. Cross the bridge and two more stiles to reach a field. A clear diagram on the fence shows the footpath around the field to a stile. Go over, then straight ahead to another stile and gate, to the left of a house. Cross the A4189, with care, go over a stile, and through a field to a stile in the top left corner. Go over and down a sunken track to another stile and bridge. Turn left and walk around the field boundary and, when another path joins from the left, turn right, uphill, to a stile. Walk between fences, cross a railway station bridge and take the signed tarmac path almost opposite, between houses, to reach the High Street. Cross, turn right, past the church, and watch for the 'Medical Centre' sign – follow this to the car park.

POINTS OF INTEREST:
Henley-in-Arden – The town was granted a charter for a weekly fair and market in 1140, and grew up along the line of Feldon Street – the old main road out of the Forest of Arden. The 15th-century Guild Hall, restored in 1915, holds a collection of civic relics including furniture, pewter plate, maces and the 1449 charter that granted privileges to the town. The Norman church of St Nicholas has one of the finest east windows in the county. In the same street is St John the Baptist Church, which is late 15th century and has a fine timber roof and an early 16th-century pulpit. The stalls and woodwork are modern.
Heart of England Way – This long distance footpath was the idea of a group of walking clubs in 1978. It was achieved through the hard work of volunteers over the next decade. They cleared and waymarked the route, which runs for 80 miles from Cannock Chase to Chipping Campden, linking the Staffordshire Way with the Cotswold Way.

REFRESHMENTS:
There is a good choice of inns and cafes in Henley-in-Arden.

Walk 67   DUDLEY AND WRENS NEST   6¹/₂m (10¹/₂km)

Maps: OS Sheets Landranger 139; Pathfinder 912. The
Birmingham A-Z is also useful.

Allow a full day for this easy walk linking gems around Dudley.
Start: At 935923, the Wrens Nest Reserve main entrance.

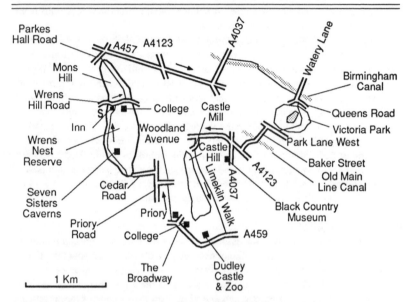

Alternative parking is available at the museum or castle for visitors.

Turn right along Wrens Hill Road, passing the college, then left along a path
through the Mons Hill area of the Reserve. When the path forks and steps go right,
keep left. Nearing houses, turn right, eventually going down steps to Parkes Hall
Road. Turn right to the A457. Turn right, go over the A4123 and left down the A4037
to the Birmingham Canal. Turn right along the towpath and at the bridge opposite the
railway signal box, turn right down Watery Lane. Cross Queens Road into Victoria
Park, passing left of the lake and tennis courts. Bear right at a fork, leave the park and
turn right into Park Lane West. Turn left into Baker Street. Cross over the Old Main
Line Canal and turn right along A4123 to reach its junction with the A4037. The
Black Country Museum entrance is left, down the road. The walk crosses to the

A4123 then turns left down Castle Mill. Take Limekiln Walk, on the left, beside Castle Hill to reach the A459. Turn right past the entrance to **Dudley Castle** and bear right up the Broadway, passing the college to reach the 12th-century Priory ruins. Foundations of the chapter house, dining hall, dormitory and central cloister, along with the chapel ruins, are all that remain.

Walk through Priory Park and turn left down Woodland Avenue. Cross Priory Road (the A4168), turn right and, shortly, left down Cedar Road to enter the southern end of **Wrens Nest** by an information board. Here you have several choices: either turn left and follow the lower path beside houses, or walk ahead and up a long flight of steps on the left to reach a higher path. This path leads north past the Seven Sisters Caverns, which can be seen safely from a viewing platform. However, *all* of the Reserve is worth exploring. As long as you keep to the left side of the Reserve and head north (trees restrict distant views so a compass is helpful), both the upper and lower paths will eventually emerge at the northern end, by Wrens Hill Road and the start.

POINTS OF INTEREST:

Black Country Museum – The museum offers a fascinating glimpse into the area's industrial past. A complete canal-side village can be seen, including a pub, shops, chapel, ironworks and houses. The Dudley Canal Trust runs boat trips into Dudley Tunnel which was part of a huge network of underground caverns, mines and basins.
Dudley Castle – This stronghold of the Earls of Dudley was used as a Royalist garrison in the Civil War. It was devastated by fire in 1750. Dudley Zoo, in the grounds, and the ruins are both popular attractions. Castle Hill was planted with trees by the Earl of Dudley in 1800 after the hillside became riddled with tunnels and caverns from limestone mining.
Wrens Nest – The area was declared a National Nature Reserve for geology in 1956. Originally limestone workings and now surrounded by housing, nature has wrought a remarkable transformation. The grassland is rich in wildflowers and the woods and scrub support a variety of birds, insects and butterflies. The outcrop of Wenlock limestone is a rich source of fossils which once lived in the Silurian sea over 420 million years ago. Finds can be seen in the Dudley museum. The town's coat of arms shows the 'Dudley Bug', a famous trilobite fossil of a type once common in the area. The site is largely stripped, so collecting is discouraged to preserve what little remains and no hammers are allowed.

REFRESHMENTS:
The Cave Inn, by the main Wrens Nest Reserve entrance.
There is a restuarant in the Black Country Museum and plenty of choice in Dudley.

Walk 68 WILMCOTE AND THE STRATFORD CANAL 7m (11km)

Maps: OS Sheets Landranger 151; Pathfinder 975, 997 and 998.
*A walk along the Stratford Canal to Wilmcote and Newnham,
with a return by public transport.*
Start: At 207548, Tourist Information Centre, Bridgefoot.

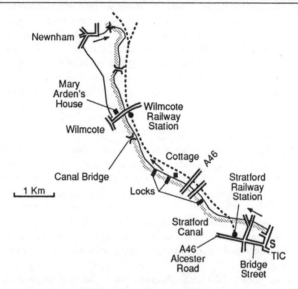

From the Stratford Tourist Information Centre at Bridgefoot, turn right over the canal bridge, and cross Guild Street at the traffic lights. Turn right (with the Red Lion Inn on the opposite side of the road). Go over Payton Street and almost immediately reach a canal bridge. Descend to the towpath on the right side of the **Stratford canal**. The path follows the right bank of the canal for the next 2 miles to Wilmcote, passing under a railway bridge, another road bridge and the first of many locks. The railway runs parallel to the canal all the way into **Wilmcote**. After reaching two more road bridges the countryside opens out and the walker passes a series of locks (there are eleven between here and Wilmcote), with cottages on the right. Care is needed on the towpath in muddy conditions. Go past another, smaller, pedestrian canal bridge and, at the next bridge, climb up into Wilmcote village. Turn left, passing Mary Arden's house on the right, to reach a T-junction by the Swan House hotel.

128

Turn right, then look for the yellow waymark opposite the post office and follow the path behind Mary Arden's House. Go over two stiles and follow the hedge on the right. After crossing two more stiles, the path is well-marked with blue arrows. Walk across a long field, parallel to a tree-lined hedge, and cross a bridleway. The path now swings left across fields, crossing four stiles, keeping the hedge on the left. Go over a stile by a gate on to a lane and turn right past Retreat Farm to reach **Newnham** village. Continue down the lane, but, on reaching a sharp left bend, leave the road, over a stile on the right, taking the left of two waymarked paths. Cross a field to a stile in a fence. Go over and cross a paddock to a stile by a junction of two hedges. Go through the hedge on the right and turn left, again following the hedge, then go right along the field edge to emerge suddenly on to the Stratford Canal towpath, going over a metal bridge. Turn right and follow the towpath for nearly 2 miles to Wilmcote, a split pedestrian bridge is passed on the way.

You can return either on the train from Wilmcote station (not available on winter Sundays) or by a frequent open top bus service from the village. The bus stops at various points in Stratford town centre, including the Tourist Information Centre at the start of the walk. If returning by train, on leaving the station turn left into the Alcester road, cross the traffic lights into Greenhill Street and walk along Wood Street and Bridge Street to reach the start.

POINTS OF INTEREST:

Stratford-upon-Avon Canal – Although open in 1816 it was bought by a railway company in 1856 and fell into disuse: by 1945 some sections were unusable. It was restored in the 1960s and now bustles with leisure boat activity. The iron bridges were split in the centre to allow horse tow ropes to pass through. The canal goes through quiet, unspoilt country, with plenty of wildlife interest.

Wilmcote – The most famous house in the village was the childhood home of Mary Arden, mother of William Shakespeare. It is now owned by the Shakespeare Birthplace Trust and is open to the public. It is a beautiful timbered building with an ancient dovecote. In the same complex is the Countryside Museum, which was a working farm until this century and now offers falconry displays.

Newnham – Now a quiet village, Newnham was the site of a quarry which supplied the stone for Clopton Bridge in Stratford-upon-Avon and for St Mary's Church in Warwick.

REFRESHMENTS:

The Masons Arms, Wilmcote.
The Swan House hotel, Wilmcote.

Walk 69   **ARROW AND WEETHLEY**   7m (11km)
Maps: OS Sheets Landranger 150; Pathfinder 997.
An undulating walk, skirting woodland, with good views and
returning past a delightful church and a stately home.
Start: At 081565, in Arrow village.

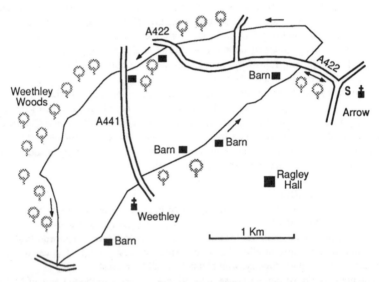

Walk along the A422, signed to Worcester, with care, and when the road clears the
trees, take the footpath on the right, alongside a hedge. Climb a stile in the top corner
and go past a metal gate to another gate. Turn left and follow the waymarked route
through two gaps. On reaching a stile and a brick footbridge, turn left and follow the
left side of the next field. Cross a farm track, maintaining direction, with a hedge on
the right, to pass a pond and wood and reach the A422 over a stile.

Cross, with care, and follow the drive to Thornhill Farm. Walk to the right of the
buildings and go through a gate on the right, at the rear of a wooden garage. Turn left,
parallel with a hedge, and climb the slope to reach a stile in the hedge on the left.
Climb past the house, going through two gates to reach the A441. The lay-by here is
an alternative start if parking is difficult in Arrow. Cross, with care, and go through a

gate opposite into a field. Now walk towards Weethley Woods, but do not enter: instead, turn left along a footpath, with woods on the right and fields on the left, following it for 2 miles. After a mile, the condition of the path, in wet weather, deteriorates as it is badly cut up by vehicles. Ignore a path, to the left, across fields, and keep wood on your right to reach a minor road.

The next path lies diagonally back across the last field walked but is not clear underfoot. If in doubt, aim for the protruding hedge corner in line with a barn, until you reach a gap in the hedge. There being no waymarking and no headland in the field on the right, the least damaging route goes left, with the hedge on the right, to skirt the left side of the barn. Turn right through a gateway and walk, with a hedge on your left, past a tree. Now aim for the churchyard, going along a faint path diagonally across a long field. St James' Church in **Weethley** hamlet is in a delightful setting with glorious views. Continue down the lane to the A441 and cross, with care, to the stile opposite. The route is now well waymarked, following the fence on the right. Go over a stile, skirt the parkland of **Ragley Hall** and go past several old barns, still keeping hedges on your right, for $1^1/_2$ miles. On reaching the A422, opposite the path used earlier, turn right to return to **Arrow**.

POINTS OF INTEREST:
Weethley – A settlement has existed here since the 8th century when it was part of the Mercian kingdom. The rebuilding of St James' Church was paid for by Henry Miles in 1857. Since before 1900, a service was held each week until 1967 when an outbreak of foot and mouth disease in the churchwarden's flock made the church inaccessible for six weeks.
Ragley Hall – This impressive Palladian mansion dates from 1680 and houses a superb collections of paintings and furniture. It is the home of the Marquess of Hertford. The original parkland was landscaped by Capability Brown, and now offers lakeside picnic areas, an adventure playground, a maze and woodland walks.
Arrow – This small group of cottages and an old toll house dates from the 1850s. The church was restored in 1863 and has a Norman doorway, with an 18th-century tower designed by Horace Walpole. A stone coffin lid, discovered during the restoration, dates from 1303 and is from the coffin of Sir Gerald de Camville who fought with Edward I in Scotland.

REFRESHMENTS:
None on the route, but there is plenty of choice in nearby Alcester.

Walk 70   AROUND MEON HILL   7m (11km)

Maps: OS Sheets Landranger 151; Pathfinder 1020.

Superb walk circling the hill and visiting two gardens. Well waymarked with many stiles.

Start: At 162436, the Memorial Fountain, Mickleton.

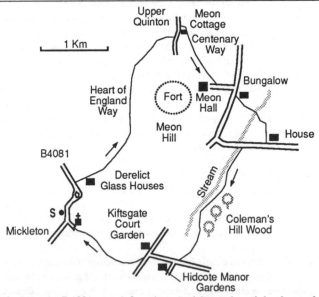

Walk left along the B4081, turn left at the roundabout, then right along a lane, past derelict glasshouses. You are now on the well-signed Heart of England Way, with **Meon Hill**, to the right. Continue to a stile, the first of 23 to be crossed! Cross a field and climb two stiles. At the next corner two stiles lead through a plantation: go over a stile and across a long field to a double stile. The path now runs along the hedge, on the left. Go over another stile and right, along the field edge, to a footbridge and two more stiles. Cross a long field, past a marker post and go over a stile into a lane. Turn left into Upper Quinton and take the Centenary Way, to the right, past Meon Cottage. Go over two stiles and turn right by a plantation. Cross another stile and follow the well-defined path diagonally left to the field's top corner. Follow the hedge on the right, past a gate, turn right and, shortly, left over two stiles. Walk straight across a

132

field to a lane near Meon Hall. Turn left to reach a road. Turn right, past a bungalow, to reach another stile, on the left. Go diagonally left across a field to a gate. Follow a hedge to a footbridge, turn right and, on reaching another hedge, go left. The path is well signed as it swings right by a tall hedge and emerges on to a minor road.

Turn right for $1/_2$ mile to a stile on the left. Cross this and a footbridge, then turn right beside a stream and climb a field towards woodland. Go over a stile into Coleman's Hill Wood, and, after the next stile, continue to another wood. At its end, cross a stile and, keeping a hedge on your right, follow a faint path across parkland. Where the hedge ends, cross diagonally right to a gate. Turn right through the car park at **Hidcote Manor Gardens** and go along a lane to a T-junction. **Kiftsgate Court Garden** is to the right here. Go through the gateway opposite, by a bridleway sign, and descend to a gateway. Take the footpath signed diagonally right, and drop downhill across fields. Now heave tired legs over two stiles (the last of the day!). St Lawrence's Church is in sight ahead as you walk across two fields and through gates to skirt the churchyard. The lane leads to **Mickleton**, with the start to the right.

POINTS OF INTEREST:

Meon Hill – The hill is topped by an Iron Age camp, but has no footpath over the summit. Numerous ghost stories are attached to the Hill – a huntsman and his hounds are said to chase a phantom fox around it and a huntsman, killed by his own hounds after hunting at night, haunts it. An unsolved mystery is the murder of a farm labourer who, in 1945, was found pinned to the ground with his own pitchfork.

Hidcote Manor Gardens – Donated to the National Trust by Major Lawrence Johnson, who created them, Hidcote consists of a series of small, individually designed gardens, each with a different theme.

Kiftsgate Court Garden – The garden is in a dramatic hillside setting and much quieter than neighbouring Hidcote.

Mickleton – A large village in an attractive setting. The 12th-century St Lawrence's Church has a striking 14th-century tower and spire, plus an unusual two-storeyed, 17th-century porch. Inside are an impressive organ in a fine wooden gallery, a 15th-century parish chest fashioned from a tree trunk and a vivid stained glass window. The 17th-century octagonal bowl of the font is beautifully carved with roses.

REFRESHMENTS:

The Kings Arms , Mickleton.
The Butchers Arms, Mickleton.
There are tea rooms at Hidcote and Kiftsgate Gardens when these are open.

Walk 71   BEAUDESERT AND LOWSONFORD   7m (11km)

Maps: OS Sheets Landranger 151; Pathfinder 975.

Walk from site of ancient castle to interesting villages and along a canal.

Start: At 153657, Prince Harry Road car park, Henley.

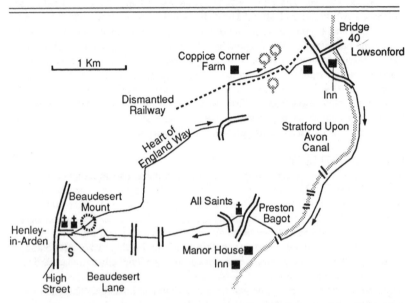

Follow the signs to the High Street in Henley-in-Arden and turn right. Go right again into Beaudesert Lane, passing two churches, and then taking a path steeply uphill on to the ramparts of **Beaudesert Mount**. The route now follows the Heart of England Way (*see* Note to Walk 66) all the way to **Lowsonford** and is well waymarked. Follow the main path over the castle site and climb the escarpment beyond, aiming for a power pole. Go over a stile on the left, keep to the top of the escarpment and, at the next stile, go right and cross a field to the stile opposite. Turn left, and at the first junction, go right over a stile and cross a field. Go over a track, then go downhill with a hedge on your left. Cross the next field via two stiles and walk with the hedge on your right towards cypress trees. Go over two stiles and continue to a farm drive, following it to a road. Turn left, and, shortly, left again up the drive towards Coppice

Corner Farm. Go over an old railway bridge and, just before the buildings, go through a gate on the right and follow the track beyond to a gateway. Turn sharp right towards a plantation, entering the trees at a marker post. Follow a well-defined path to a stile on the far side. Keep to the right edge of the field beyond, cross two stiles and turn right. Just beyond another old railway bridge, turn left over a stile and cross two fields to reach a lane by a house. Turn left to a crossroads in Lowsonford.

Go down the lane opposite to bridge No. 40 on the Stratford-upon-Avon canal (*see* Note to Walk 68). Turn right (south) along the towpath as far as the fifth bridge (unnumbered but by Lock 36). Turn right across a metal footbridge and go over a stile into a large field. Climb by the left hedge, go through a gateway and aim slightly left of the church to reach a stile. Go through the handgate opposite to All Saints' Church, **Preston Bagot**. Beyond the church, go through a gate and downhill to a minor road. Go through the gateway opposite into a field, and walk ahead to reach a stile. The path beyond is waymarked across several fields, following the hedge on the right. On reaching a farm track, go slightly right, then left across fields to a lane. Cross, and walk with a hedge on your right. Cross two stiles and drop steeply downhill to playing fields. Go through a gate and along an alleyway, across several streets and by a school, to reach Beaudesert Lane. At its end, turn left into the High Street.

POINTS OF INTEREST:
Beaudesert Mount – A marvellous viewpoint and the site of a 12th-century motte and bailey castle of the De Montforts. The lord of the manor, Peter de Montfort, backed his cousin, Simon de Montfort in his rebellion against Henry III. Peter fought and died alongside Simon in the Battle of Evesham in 1265 and the castle was partly destroyed in the reprisals that followed. Little remains except the rounded hilltop and ditches which mark the site of the former moat.
Preston Bagot – This small village has a beautiful 16th-century, half-timbered manor house. The Norman All Saints' Church stands on a hilltop and at certain times of the year the setting sun strikes the altar cross in a blaze of light. The neo-Norman chancel was added around 1870. It was designed by J.A. Chatwin, a local architect who also designed the chancel in Birmingham Cathedral.
Lowsonford – The hamlet was once known as Lonesomeford. On the canal is a picturesque barrel-roofed cottage.

REFRESHMENTS:
The Crab Mill , Preston Bagot.
The Haven Tea Rooms, Preston Bagot.
The Fleur dy Lys Inn, Lowsonford.

Walk 72   WOMBORNE AND BAGGERIDGE   7m (11km)

Maps: OS Sheets Landranger 139; Pathfinder 912.

A country park, a disused railway and interesting villages on a marvellous walk.

Start: At 898931, the Visitor Centre car park.

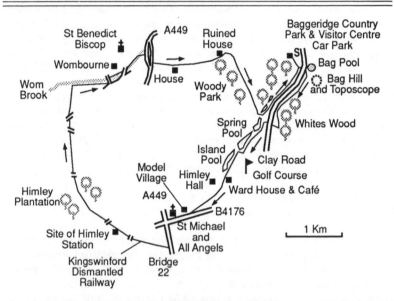

From the Centre, walk through the overflow car park and down steps. Turn left under a bridge, then turn right past Bag Pool, keeping right along a surfaced path. A detour uphill to the toposcope on Bag Hill is recommended for the wonderful views to the Wrekin, Clee Hills, Malverns and beyond. Now keep a clay road to the right, go right at a path fork and straight over at a junction. At the next crossroads, turn right into Whites Wood, over a bridleway ahead. On reaching conifers, turn right under a bridge, then turn left, downhill, to join a path beside Spring Pool. Walk with the park fence and a golf course on the left, passing Island Pool, at the end of which leave the park and turn left down a lane. Walk past Rock Pool to reach Himley Hall Park. Go past Ward House, turning left, then right through a car park to reach a gateway by the model village and miniature railway. Turn right, with care, along the B4176, passing

136

St Michael and All Angels' Church. At the traffic lights, turn left along the A449, again with care, to Bridge 22 of the **Kingswinford Railway Walk**. Turn right (north) along the railway, passing the site of Himley station and going through the Woodland Trust's Himley Plantation. After the fifth bridge, (No. 29), turn right down a path to Wom Brook. Turn right and follow the path to a road at Gravel Hill. Go left over the footbridge to the road. Turn right, and shortly left, to rejoin the path by the brook. Cross Mill lane (where access to **Wombourne** village centre is possible), continuing along the path by the brook to reach a road by the Red Lion.

Turn right, but just before the end of the road, turn left, cross the busy A449, with care, using an unusual stile in the central reservation. Go through a kissing gate, up a green lane and past a house. Walk up the left edge of the field, under pylons, to reach a wood. Go half-left, along a waymarked path, passing a ruined house and walls. Emerge from the trees and cross a field, turning right along a track before woodland. Follow the track, with the woods of Woody Park on the right, downhill, by a wall. Go through an old estate gateway, and cross a stile and footbridge to re-enter **Baggeridge Country Park**. Turn left and follow the main gravel path past the pools and up through woodland to the start.

POINTS OF INTEREST:

Kingswinford Railway Walk – This $5\frac{1}{2}$ mile linear walk follows the line of a disused railway. The single track Kingswinford Branch Railway opened in 1925 to connect Wolverhampton with Kingswinford, but services were withdrawn in 1932. Himley station was built for the convenience of the Earl of Dudley and his guests.

Wombourne – The name derives from the Wom Brook which flows through the centre. The green is now used by the local cricket, tennis and bowling clubs. The present church of St Benedict Biscop dates from around 1400 – though most was built in the late 1800s – and is on the site of an earlier building constructed in 1086.

Baggeridge Country Park – The Parkland was once part of the Himley Hall estate. Coal production ceased in 1968 and it was designated a Country Park in 1970. Reclamation work, including the planting of 20,000 trees and shrubs, was completed over the next decade, with the park opening in 1983. Whites Wood has sycamore and birch and, in the Spring, bluebells, wood anemones and wood sorrel thrive. The pools were created in the mid-18th century. Fragile heath and grassland support many species of butterfly, including Meadow Brown, Gatekeeper and Small Heath.

REFRESHMENTS:

There is a cafe in Himley Hall Park.

There is also plenty of choice in Wombourne.

Walk 73 LONG ITCHINGTON AND BASCOTE LOCKS 7m (11km)
Maps: OS Sheets Landranger 151; Pathfinder 977 and 976.
A Figure of Eight walk, from a charming village and along a canal.
Start: At 414653, the village green, Long Itchington.

No one will go thirsty (or hungry) on this walk which passes by seven inns!

From the village green and pond, walk down Church Road and turn right, past a yellow arrow by the bus stop. This path, part of the Village Nature Trail, leads past the cemetery to go between the backs of houses in Church Road and the rear of Galanos House. Turn left through a gate into Orchard Way, emerging again into Church Road. Turn left, and then right down Bascote Road. Cross the bridge over the River Itchen and soon, climb over a stile on the right into a field, joining part of the Bascote Nature Trail. Follow the hedge on the left to go over another stile. Notice the helpful signs indicating where the footpaths traverse the next field – would that all paths were so clearly marked! Climb up the pasture, with the hedge on your left, and through a kissing gate. Cross the dismantled railway via steps and another kissing gate. White's

138

Spinney now lies to the right with a mix of lime, oak, elms, cherry and field maple. Keep ahead to emerge into a large field. Unfortunately the clear path now disappears and, at the time of writing, the path was ploughed up. The path should cross the centre of the field and drop towards the hedge at the bottom, where a gap leads to a road. If the way is still unclear, take the path which has developed around the left edge of the field to reach the gap. Turn right to reach Bridge 27 of the Grand Union Canal (*see* Note to Walk 5).

Turn right along the towpath, passing Bascote locks to reach Bridge 30. Now leave the canal, going over the bridge and following the road for almost a mile. Go past the first farm drive, turning left at the next, signed to Bascote Lodge Farm. Although not waymarked, this bridleway joins a lane by farm buildings. Turn right to reach a T-junction. Turn left into Bascote and stay on the road to reach Bridge 27, where the Grand Union Canal is rejoined. Turn right along the towpath for two miles passing the junction with the A423 (where a short cut to **Long Itchington** is possible). At Bridge 23, by the Blue Lias Inn, and just before the Stockton Flight, turn left along Stockton road, passing Feldon Middle School. Turn right at the A423 T-junction and then left to reach the village green.

POINTS OF INTEREST:
Long Itchington – This charming village has a 12th-century church (Holy Trinity) on the bank of the River Itchen. Sandstone buttresses support the tower. The top of the spire was blown down in 1762 and only a stump remains. Inside is a 14th-century rood screen and stone seats in the chancel for use by the priests during Mass. St Wulfstan, Bishop of Worcester, is believed to have been born in the village in the 11th century. The Tudor House on the green, home of Lady Holbourne, hosted visits by Elizabeth I in 1572 and 1575. An informative Nature Trail booklet is produced by the 'Alive' Project (Annual Long Itchington Venture for the Environment). It details three walks centred on the village. The project is aimed at encouraging villagers to become involved in their local environment. Previous worthwhile initiatives have included clearing White's Spinney, creating a Nature Reserve and cleaning up the village.

REFRESHMENTS:
The Blue Lias, near Stockton Locks.
Two Boats Inn and *Cuttle Inn*, on the canal by the A423.
There are also four inns in Long Itchington.

Walk 74 CRACKLEY WOOD AND KENILWORTH 7¹/₂m (12km)

Maps: OS Sheets Landranger 140; Pathfinder 955.

A wonderful walk, perfect for spring and autumn. Can be muddy.

Start: At 286724, Abbey Fields car park.

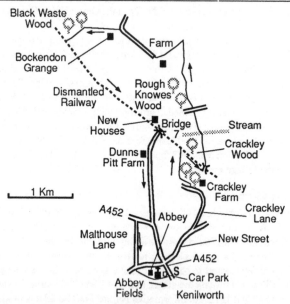

Turn left from the car park, following the A452, with care, into Old Kenilworth. Turn right at the traffic lights into New Street. After ¹/₂ mile, take the second turning on the left, Crackley Lane. Go past the drive to Crackley Farm (where a short cut to the railway bridge is possible), and at the lay-by, go through the barrier into **Crackley Wood**. Numerous paths criss-cross the wood: stay on the path running parallel to the wood's left edge to eventually reach a **disused railway**. Turn right along the old line as far as the first bridge. Climb up and turn left across the bridge. Go through the gate ahead and follow the well-defined bridleway beyond along the left edge of a field. Go through another gate to ford the stream.

Climb uphill, cross a road and go ahead along a fenced path, with Roughknowles Wood on the left. Descend a field and go through a gate. Ignore the bridleway beyond, going over the stile on the right. Cross a field diagonally to reach another stile. Go over and turn half-left, aiming for a stile to the left of a lone tree. Go over and follow the hedge on the right, swinging left with it to reach a road at the end of the field. Turn right. At a sharp right bend, go over the stile opposite, to the right of Bockendon Grange Drive, and follow the hedge on the right over two stiles. Ignore a stile on the right and walk along the edge of Black Waste Wood, the hedge swinging left to cross a brook. Climb a stile and walk ahead to meet the dismantled railway line again.

Turn left, go under a bridge and past new houses to reach Bridge 7. Leave the old railway here, down steep steps on the far side, and turn left (south) down a lane, passing Dunns Pitts Farm to reach the A452. Turn right, and then left at the first turning, Malthouse Lane. At the lane's end, turn left, and almost immediately right into Abbey Fields. The lake ahead is home to a healthy population of wildfowl which breed unperturbed amid the bustle of the park. Keep on the main path, with the lake on your right, to pass the remains of the **Abbey**. The car park is beyond **St Nicholas' Church**.

POINTS OF INTEREST:

Crackley Wood – Carpeted with bluebells in the spring, the open glades encourage a wealth of wild flowers, butterflies and birds. Trees include beech, sweet chestnut, birch, oak, rowan, hazel and holly with a plantation of sycamore and larch. Holly Blue, Speckled Wood, Green-veined White and Tortoiseshell butterflies thrive, while covering the woodland floor are herb robert, pink campion, wild roses, ox-eye daisies, buttercups and clover.

Disused Railway – Built in 1848 to link Berkswell and Kenilworth, the track was removed in 1969 and the line is now a popular local walk.

Abbey of St Mary the Virgin – The abbey was founded in 1122 by Geoffrey de Clinton as a priory for Augustinian Canons. Damaged by the King's soldiers during the siege of the castle in 1207, it was finally dissolved in 1538. Subsequently, stone from the abbey was used in repairs to the castle so that little remains except a gatehouse and a tithe barn. Churchyard extensions revealed the full size of the abbey church: at 160 feet long it was one of the largest of its kind in the country.

St Nicholas' Church – The pulpit, screen and lectern are examples of modern 20th-century carving. The west entrance was the porch to the abbey. In the chancel is a pig of lead, weighing nearly 11 hundredweight and bearing the stamp of Henry VIII's commissioner: this came from the abbey roof which was melted down during the demolition of the abbey.

REFRESHMENTS:
The Virgins and Castle Inn, Old Kenilworth.
The Royal Oak, Old Kenilworth.

Walk 75   **SOUTHAM AND UFTON**   7¹/₂m (12km)

Maps: OS Sheets Landranger 151; Pathfinder 976 and 977.

A nature reserve is the high point. Paths by a landfill the low points.

Start: At 419621, Wood Street car park, Southam.

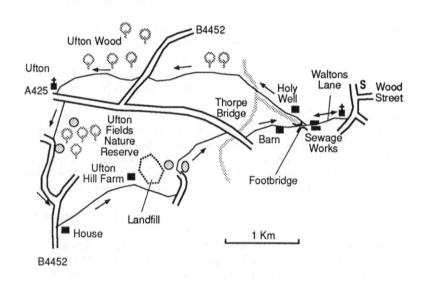

Turn right, then left into High Street and right down Park Lane to the church. Turn right by the church door and cross the recreation ground. Turn left down Walton's Lane, swinging right between the sewage works. Go over a stile and cross to the top right corner of the field ahead. The footbridge is on the return path: for now, keep the river on your left to reach the Holy Well. Two kissing gates lead into a field: go straight across two fields to a double stile. Aim half-right to a stile in a hedge, then go along an avenue of trees to a bridge over a weir. Keep the hedge on the left to reach a stile with 3 arrows. (The arrow half-left is wrong). Go straight ahead, with a hedge on your right, over a stile, then half-left to a corner by a redundant stile. Now keep a hedge on your left and go through the wood to a gate on the far side. Keep a hedge on your left and cross three fields to the B4452. Turn right, and shortly left, keeping

Ufton Wood on your right to cross two fields. After the second stile, aim towards a stile in the top left corner, by a gate. The gate ahead leads to White Hart Lane: turn left to the A425 at **Ufton**. Turn left, with care, and by the last house on the right, join the Centenary Way, passing the house and allotments. Keep a hedge on your right to reach a stile into **Ufton Fields Nature Reserve**.

Turn right, through a gate, and keep right at a path junction. At the next junction, leave the Reserve (and the Centenary Way), turning left along a road to the B4452. Turn right, and then left along a path just before the first house on the left. Head for a stile in the top right corner, then walk with a hedge on your left to another stile. Cross the long field beyond, with a hedge on the right, to a gate by Ufton Hill Farm. Keep the farm and fence on your left to the top left corner of the field, then aim for the stile in the top left corner of the next field, by the landfill. Keep a fence on your left to another stile., then join a dirt track going left. Swing right before a gate along a muddy path between ponds to reach scrubland. Go straight ahead, over a stile (ignore the arrow – it is wrong) and keep a hedge on your left beside a new plantation. Where the hedge turns left, keep straight on through a gateway into the next field. At the field end is the A425: turn right, with care, over Thorpe Bridge and go left through two gates. Bear half-right, through the trees, to a stile in the top corner. Pass a ruined barn, cross a stile and aim for the bottom left corner of a field. Cross a footbridge to rejoin the outward path and retrace it back to **Southam**.

POINTS OF INTEREST:
Ufton – A Saxon church stood on the site of St Michael's and All Angels Church as far back as 1042. Balliol College, Oxford was the church's landlord until the 1920s.
Ufton Fields Nature Reserve – Pools from old limestone workings form the Warwickshire Wildlife Trust reserve, which supports a wealth of wildlife including over 130 species of birds. Five varieties of orchid and six species of dragonfly are found here. Open to members at all times, but to the public only on Sundays.
Southam – Legend has it that Charles I stayed here after Edge Hill. He ordered the local nobles to bring their silverware to what is now The Old Mint Inn, to be converted into coins to pay his troops. The 14th-century St James' Church, built to replace an earlier one, has a 126 foot spire with four clock faces. Inside are the remains of a Tudor painting and a Jacobean pulpit. The churchyard has graves commemorating the fallen of the Crimean War.

REFRESHMENTS:
The White Hart Inn, Ufton.
There are also a tea rooms in Ufton and plenty of choice in Southam.

Walk 76   CHERINGTON AND WHICHFORD   7¹/₂m (12km)

Maps: OS Sheets Landranger 151; Pathfinder 1044.

Fine views, delightful villages and magnificent woodland feature in this enjoyable walk. Not well waymarked.

Start: At 292367, Cherington Church.

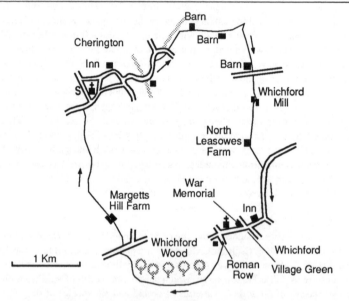

There is limited parking in the lane beyond the church but please do not obstruct gateways.

Walk past the church, on the left, and turn left at a T-junction. Ignore Featherbed Lane and continue along the road to a staggered crossroads. Turn left, and immediately right down the lane signed to Brailes. Follow the lane over a brook and past a large house, and go over a stile on the right. Go diagonally across a field to a lane. Cross and go over the stile opposite. Now keep a brook on your left to reach a stile. Turn right along the track, passing a barn. Go through a rickety gate and climb the slope ahead past another barn. At the top, where the track swings left, turn right, with a hedge on your left, to reach a footbridge in the top left corner. Head straight across the next field, swinging half-right at the corner and dropping down past barns to a lane.

144

Go ahead down the lane to Whichford Mill. Pass between the buildings on to a path between hedges. Go through a gate and follow the clear path ahead to join a lane by North Leasows Farm.

Turn left to a junction and turn right down the hill. Turn right at a junction, to **Whichford**, passing the village green and ignoring all left turns. Go left of the War Memorial and along a lane past the church. Where the road swings sharp right, turn left down Roman Row, past a new housing estate. At the end, go over a stile and ignore the path straight on, swinging right, uphill, and aiming for a corner of the woodland. This well-defined path becomes enclosed for a short distance before reaching a large field: turn right and keep the edge of **Whichford Wood** on your right to cross several fields. After a mile the track swings right, downhill, through the woodland edge, before veering left, uphill, to reach a minor road.

Turn right and, shortly, left along an unmade lane to Margetts Hill Farm (not signposted). Go between the buildings to reach a path and keep a hedge on your left to the end of the field. Go through a gap and maintain direction to reach gates at the bottom. Go through the right-hand gate and keep a hedge on your left along a wide headland. The path swings right, and then goes sharp left at a gap: stay on it, with a hedge on your right, to go through a gateway and across two fields to reach a T-junction by the postbox in **Cherington**. A right turn leads back to the church.

POINTS OF INTEREST:

Whichford – St Michael's Church has a Norman south doorway and a 14th-century tower. The organ was restored in 1927 by Lemuel Welles of New York in memory of his ancestor, who was the Governor of Connecticut in 1655. Inside is an unusual monument to John Mertun, Rector of Whichford in the early 1500s. On his tomb is an open book and a pair of glasses, thought to be one of the first carved representations of spectacles.

Whichford Wood – This beautiful, mixed woodland is a haven for birds and insects. In Spring it is a stunning sight, with bluebells carpeting the floor. Other flowers, which grow in profusion, include herb robert, pink campion and speedwell.

Cherington – The 13th-century church of St John the Baptist is full of interest, with a richly carved Jacobean altar table, a lovely 14th-century canopied tomb chest and the effigy of an unknown civilian in the nave.

REFRESHMENTS:
The Cherington Arms, Cherington.
The Norman Knight, Whichford.

Walk 77   **YARNINGALE COMMON**   7½m (12km)

Maps: OS Sheets Landranger 151; Pathfinder 975.

An undulating walk, over common, alongside a canal and through fields to Claverdon.

Start: At 189658, a road junction, Yarningale Common.

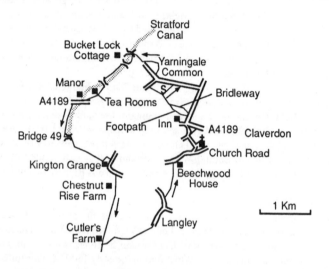

Take any of the three paths to the right of the parking area, going uphill to cross straight over the plateau. Descend on to a path through wooden barriers. This path joins another and then drops to a gravel lane: turn left and then right down a tarmac lane. At the lane's end, go along a path to the right of a house to reach the Stratford Canal (*see* Note to Walk 68). Turn left, cross a bridge to reach the towpath by Bucket Lock cottage, and turn left along it for nearly 2 miles, passing the Tea Rooms and going under the A4189.

At bridge No. 49, go left, across the bridge, and over a stile. Go diagonally right across the field beyond and through a gateway. Walk ahead, passing a power pole, and going through another gateway. Go up an enclosed path, through a gateway and, before a farm, turn left along a fence. Halfway along, go over a stile on the right and head towards a stile. Go over on to a road and turn right along it, passing Kington

146

Grange. Turn right up a lane past a new estate and then left along a bridleway past Chestnut Rise Farm.

Follow the bridleway for a mile, then, just before Cutler's Farm, turn left along a signed bridleway. Keep a wood on your left, and at its end keep right, through a gateway, following the bridleway into Langley. Continue ahead along a minor road. Ignore a right turn, taking the lane on the left. Go right down a driveway to reach a footpath and go along the enclosed track, crossing two stiles and following the hedgerow on the left to a footbridge. Cross and walk with a fence on your right, going uphill to reach a road by Beechwood House. Turn right into **Claverdon**.

Ignore a left turn, continuing along Church Road. At the back of the churchyard, go through two kissing gates and turn left into St Michael's Close. Turn right along St Michael's Road to a T-junction. Turn right and, at a left bend, cross the playing field to reach the A4189. Turn left, with care, to a crossroads. Go right up Lye Green Road and, just past the houses, take a footpath on the left. (This path and the bridleway further along the road are muddy in winter and overgrown in summer. If either is impassable, stay on the road and turn left to **Yarningale Common**.) The footpath and bridleway join up beyond a broken footbridge: keep left along the muddy path to a T-junction. Turn right, uphill. (This path is also muddy and can be avoided by taking the footpath opposite.) Where the bridleway joins a lane, turn left to return to the Common.

POINTS OF INTEREST:

Claverdon – Mentioned in the Domesday Book as Clavendone, a settlement has existed here since before Norman times. The 17th-century Forge, with its horseshoe-shaped archway, is much photographed. The Stone House was built in the 16th century by Thomas Spencer, whose tomb is in the hilltop church of St Michael and All Angels. Rebuilt in 1877, when a north aisle, organ chamber and a south chapel were added, it has a perpendicular tower and a chancel arch of the Decorated period. In the Church Centre is a large embroidered panel depicting village life in 1980. Sir Francis Gibbon, a cousin of Charles Darwin and the inventor of fingerprint identification, is buried in the churchyard.

Yarningale Common – The Common is mentioned in a land deed of 1482 and was given to Claverdon Parish Council in 1950 by the Lord of the Manor. Dominated by oak woodland, it also has remnants of heath, grassland and scrub.

REFRESHMENTS:
The Crown Inn, Claverdon.
The Haven Tea Rooms, on the canal.

Walk 78 WARMINGTON, RATLEY AND HORNTON $7\frac{1}{2}$m (12km)

Maps: OS Sheets Landranger 151; Pathfinder 1021 and 1022.
A strenuous, hilly walk linking delightful villages.
Start: At 413477, Warmington village green.

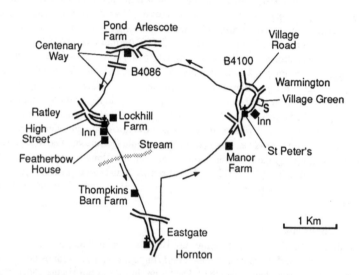

Go through the village (with the duck pond to the right), turn left down Village Road and left again along the B4100. Go right through two gates and follow a path on to a grassy terrace. Cross a stile and go along the left field edge. Cross a bridge, turn left over a stile and then right, along the field. Go through a hedgerow and straight across the field beyond, to walk by the right hedge. Turn right at the end, then left to reach a metal gate. Walk ahead to reach a stile by a pond, then keep a hedge on your right to reach a stile in the corner, by another pond. Go right, and immediate left, into **Arlescote**.

Turn left along the lane, passing a phone box and Pond Farm to reach the Centenary Way (*see* Note to Walk 34) on the left. This section of the Way is ill-defined, so be careful. Go over the fence and uphill to a metal gate. Go through and turn right immediately through another gate. Turn left, uphill, and, almost at the top, veer right to a stile. Cross this and the B4086 into a field. Go downhill, cross a footbridge

148

and aim for the top left corner of the field. Negotiate a broken fence and aim for the top left corner of the next field. Go up the lane beyond, turning left at the crossroads along the bottom road, High Street, into **Ratley**. Swing left into Church Street, passing the church and inn on the right, to follow a No-Through Road. Ignore Lockhill Farm drive, turning right past Featherbow House and following the lane to reach a stile on the right. Drop down a long field to a stile by a gate. Maintain direction to reach a gate by a stream and ditch. Keep ahead, across the stream and through another gate, then walk parallel to the hedge on the left, climbing uphill to join a track which swings right. Another path joins from the left: continue through Thompkins Barn Farm to reach a road. **Hornton** lies straight across and down the hill.

Turn left into Eastgate, passing a phonebox, and go left between Cromwells and Pear Tree Cottage. Go over a stile into a garden and walk ahead to a gate into a field. Head for a stile in the top left corner, then swing right, following the paddock fence. Follow the fence ahead to a road. Cross and follow the bridleway opposite for almost two miles, passing Manor Farm, to reach the B4100. Cross the busy junction, with care, and go left to St Peter's Church. Paths to the right of the lych-gate or at the rear of the churchyard lead back to **Warmington**.

POINTS OF INTEREST:
Arlescote – The hamlet has an old Quaker meeting house and a Tudor manor house where Charles I's two sons were housed on the night of the Civil War battle.
Ratley – Little remains of Nadbury Camp, a nearby Iron Age hillfort where excavations have revealed skeletons and weaponry. The castle, of which only earthworks remain, is thought to date from 1140. Disused by the 13th century, it was excavated in the late 1960's. St Peter ad Vincula Church contains a large stone and marble reredos, a 13th-century chancel and a 12th-century preaching cross. One of the brass memorial plates mistakenly records the age of the heiress of Simon Bury as 1697!
Hornton – This small, pleasant village has a trim green, thatched cottages and a 17th-century manor house. It was once famous for its building stone, but the nearby quarries are now closed. A mediaeval Doom painting hangs in the 12th-century church.
Warmington – A possible casualty of the battle of Edgehill, Captain Gourdin, is buried, in a grave dated October 1642, in the churchyard of the 700 year old St Michael's Church.

REFRESHMENTS:
The Plough Inn, Warmington.
The Rose and Crown, Ratley.
The Dun Cow, Hornton.

Walk 79   **CALDECOTE AND WEDDINGTON**   7¹/₂m (12km)
Maps: OS Sheets Landranger 140; Pathfinder 914.
A well waymarked walk by fields and a canal – plus plenty for railway enthusiasts!
Start: At 340933, the Poors Piece Reserve car park.

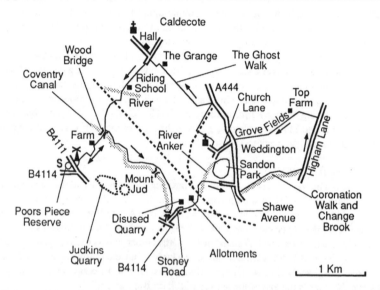

The car park is tucked away at the junction of Mancetter road (B4111) and Camp Hill road (B4114).

Turn right out of the car park and cross to a footpath. Go past a disused windmill and walk downhill. Nearby is Mount Jud – Warwickshire's only 'mountain' – in reality a 508 foot spoil heap from the old Judkins quarry! At the bottom of the hill, turn left and, shortly, right along a farm track to Wood Bridge on the Coventry Canal. Turn right along the towpath for 1¹/₂ miles, leaving at the first road bridge to turn left along the B4114.

Immediately turn left again into Stoney Road, passing houses and disused quarry buildings, then turning right over a bridge. Walk past allotments and, level with a long footbridge, turn left to go *under* the railway. On no account cross the main line

150

tracks. Here you will see 'Your Green Track' marker posts – a worthwhile attempt by the local Council to promote footpaths around Nuneaton and Bedworth. Continue beside the River Anker, turning right over a footbridge into Sandon Park in **Weddington**. Go through the car park and along Shawe Avenue to a T-junction with the A444. Turn right, then left, with care, down Coronation Walk. At the end, turn left down Higham Lane and then left down the lane to Top Farm. Turn left, before the farm buildings, to follow a bridleway which leads to Grove Fields. Cross the A444, with care, and go down Church Lane to join a bridleway to the right of the church.

Turn left alongside the churchyard, go through a gate ahead and under the railway bridge. Climb steps to the disused railway, formerly the Ashby to Nuneaton line and now the Weddington Country Walk, opened in 1983. Turn left (north) along the line to its junction with the A444. Turn left and shortly left again, crossing a field to a gap in the hedge. Turn left, and then right to follow the fence on the right. At the end of the field, keep ahead along a farm track which is known locally as the Ghost Walk, following the tragic killing of two lovers in 1832. Swing left before the Grange to reach a gate on to a drive. Turn left down the farm lane, passing the grounds of Caldecote Hall. An apology sign on a pole from 'Mountain Biking UK' may amuse. They obviously recommended this *footpath* to cyclists but were forced to retract. Keep along the lane, passing a riding school, crossing the river and going under the railway. The lane eventually reaches the canal bridge and rejoins the outward path which is reversed to the start.

POINTS OF INTEREST:
Caldecote – The nave and chancel of St Theobald and St Chad's Church were restored in the 1850's. The only features remaining from the 13th century are fragments of old glass and the south door with its scroll hinges. Inside can be found monuments to the Purefoy family. Access to the church is by kind permission of the owner. Caldecote Hall was the home of Colonel Purefoy, a supporter of Oliver Cromwell. The Hall was beseiged in 1642 during the Civil War. Later it was partly destroyed by fire, the current building being constructed in 1880.
Weddington – This was an isolated farming village before the 1930's, but has since spread to join Nuneaton, St James' Church being the only old building remaining. Rebuilt after a fire in 1733, it has a medieval north transept, now used as a vestry. Allotments occupy the site of the 16th-century castle which, after use as a Red Cross hospital in World War I, was converted into flats, but demolished in 1928.

REFRESHMENTS:
None on the route, but there is plenty of choice in nearby Nuneaton.

Walk 80   STOCKTON AND CALCUTT LOCKS   7¹/₂m (12km)
Maps: OS Sheets Landranger 151; Pathfinder 977.
A pleasant walk across farmland and along a delightful canal.
Crops can obscure footpaths.
Start: At 426648, the lay-by beyond the canal bridge.

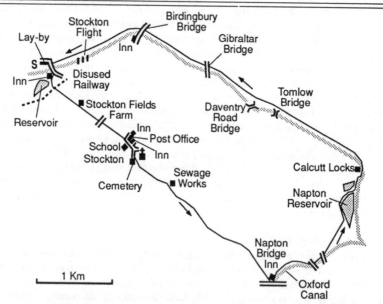

Go down the minor road, over the canal bridge and turn right into the drive of the Blue Lias Inn. Walk ahead down a track through the fishermen's car park, and along the left edge of the reservoir. At the corner, go through kissing gates either side of the old railway and along a path by a young plantation. Go over a stile and follow the hedge on the right to go through a gap at the field end. Now follow the hedge on the left until the path swings left, then go over a stile on the right. Follow the enclosed path beyond past Stockton Fields Farm and walk alongside a hedge to reach a road. Cross the road and the stile opposite and follow the hedge on the right to the corner. Go over two stiles and go left up an alleyway into **Stockton**.

Go straight ahead at the first crossroads to reach a T-junction by the Post Office. Turn right, past the school, and take the lane on the right, beside the church. Walk past houses, then swing right before a barn to pass a cemetery. Stay on the farm track to reach a T-junction. Climb the gate ahead and aim for a gap in the top left corner by a sewage works. Go through and turn half-right to reach a stile by twin power poles. (At the time of writing, no path exists in the next few fields and the going is difficult when crops are high. Any help in defining a path, as others have tried to do, will be appreciated by future walkers). Cross straight over the field to a gate, go through and head for the top left corner of the next field. Go over a stile and head across the middle of the next two fields (following vehicle tracks as best you can) to reach a gap a third of the way in from the top left corner of the next field. Now go half-left and aim for a stile in the hedge ahead, by two trees. Go over and follow the fence on the right across two fields to reach the Napton Bridge Inn.

Turn left along the towpath of the Oxford Canal (*see* Note to Walk 8). At the second bridge, take a path on the left which heads diagonally left over three fields to reach **Napton Reservoir**. Walk left around the reservoir and go over a footbridge to the Grand Union Canal (*see* Note to Walk 5). Turn left, cross plank bridges and a lock gate, then go left again along the towpath on the opposite bank. Follow the towpath for over three miles, eventually passing Stockton Flight, a group of ten locks altered in the late 1920s, where the original narrow locks act as overspill weirs alongside the new ones. Leave the canal at the bridge beyond the flight to return to the start.

POINTS OF INTEREST:

Stockton – This was a tiny hamlet until the 19th century when the famous Blue Lias clay was discovered. Since then vast quantities of cement have been extracted. Victoria Embankment in London is the most famous construction made out of this cement. Fortunately the quarries are well away from the village. A 20 million year old fossil of an ichthyosaurus was found in the quarries. St Michael's Church has a perpendicular 15th-century sandstone tower, while the rest of the building comprises a mixture of sandstone and local stone. The chancel has some 14th-century features.

Napton Reservoir – The reservoir provides plenty of wildlife interest with breeding birds such as mallard, coot and great crested grebe. Other birds which may be seen include heron, pied wagtail and little grebe, while various species of dragonfly abound.

REFRESHMENTS:
The Blue Lias Inn, near Stockton Flight locks.
The Boat Inn, lies off the canal on the A426.
The Crown Inn, Stockton.
The Barley Mow, Stockton.
Napton Bridge Inn, by the canal on the A425.

Walk 81   MERIDEN AND CLOSE WOOD   8m (13km)

Maps: OS Sheets Landranger 139; Pathfinder 935.

A walk from the 'centre' of England, across farmland to skirt woodland.

Start: At 238823, the village green, Meriden.

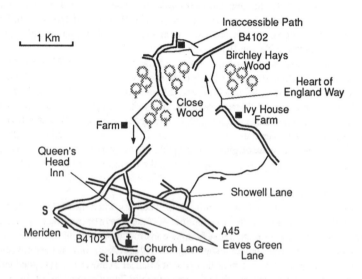

With the shops on your left, walk eastwards, up the B4102, for a mile in the direction of Coventry, then turn left down the Old Road, signed to the Queen's Head. The turning opposite is Church Lane, which leads to the impressive church. Go past the inn and follow Eaves Green Lane, left, ignoring Walsh Lane on the left, to walk under the A45, turning right into Showell Lane. Ignore the first footpath (the Heart of England Way) on the left, taking the next path on the left, by the large boulders. This bridleway leads to a minor road, after about a mile. Turn left along the road, passing Ivy House Farm to reach the **Heart of England Way** on the right. Follow the Way across a field to a footbridge, cross and continue to Birchley Hays Wood. Turn left along the edge of the wood and the next field to reach a gateway, still following the Heart of England Way.

Turn left and go through the first gateway on the right. Cross the centre of a muddy field, go over a stile and walk along the right edge of a field to another stile. At this point, do not go over the stile: instead, leave the well-marked Heart of England Way by turning left. Although, according to the OS map, there are several footpaths across these fields, no marker posts or paths can be seen. The public rights of way to the right of the house on the left are not accessible and there are no arrows to indicate the path across the fields on the left. The best way lies left, with the hedge on your right, passing through a gateway. Now keep to the right edge of the next field aiming for the field bottom. Just to the right of a house in the bottom left corner, you will finally find a stile and a marker post: go over on to a road. Turn left along the road to go through Close Wood. At the wood's end, climb a stile on the right, by a pond, and walk ahead, with the wood on your right. Climb another stile, and at the end of the next field, go over a stile into a conifer plantation.

Keep to the main path straight through the plantation and go over a stile on the far side. Walk straight across the next field to emerge between the barn and house. Turn left along the farm lane, following it to the B4102. Turn right, with care, to reach the roundabout in **Meriden**.

POINTS OF INTEREST:
Heart of England Way – This long distance footpath was the idea of a group of walking clubs in 1978. It was achieved through the hard work of volunteers over the next decade. They cleared and waymarked the route, which runs for 80 miles from Cannock Chase to Chipping Campden, linking the Staffordshire Way with the Cotswold Way.
Meriden – This pleasant commuter village is one of several claimants to the title of the centre of England. In support of the claim there is a cross on the village green with the inscription 'This ancient wayside cross has stood in the village for some 500 years and by tradition marks the Centre of England. The cross was rebuilt on this site when the green was improved in celebration of the Festival of Britain, 1951'. Also on the green is a memorial pillar 'in remembrance of those cyclists who gave their lives in World War Two'. The Church of St Lawrence, founded by Lady Godiva and situated outside the village, has a partly Norman chancel, gargoyles on the tower and a golden weathercock. The nave is lit by early 19th-century Perpendicular windows. The outer walls of the aisle were rebuilt in the 19th century with the vestry added later.

REFRESHMENTS:
The Queen's Head, Meriden.
The Bull's Head, Meriden.

Walk 82   **ALVECOTE POOLS AND POLESWORTH**   8m (13km)
Maps: OS Sheets Landranger 139 and 140; Pathfinder 893.
Ideal for bird watchers and train enthusiasts! Some road walking.
Start: At 252043, the picnic area at Alvecote Priory.

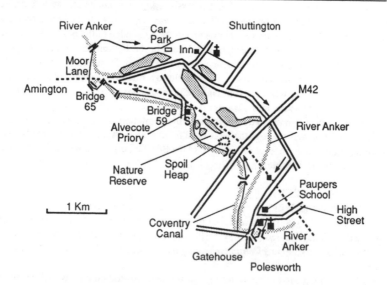

From **Alvecote Priory** car park, turn right to reach canal Bridge 59. Turn left (westwards) along the towpath of the Coventry Canal to reach Bridge 65. Turn right to the green in Amington, going right into Moor Lane, by Langdale Court, and over the railway bridge. Continue ahead to a stile, cross the field beyond to its top right corner and go over a footbridge (planks missing) across the River Anker. Do not go over the stile immediately ahead: instead, follow the hedge on the right to a farm drive. Go over a stile and turn right, with the hedge on your right, to follow the headland right, and then left, to a stile by a gate. Go ahead, with a fence on your left, but when it turns left, keep straight on past an oak and a pile of rubble (once Warren Farm). Keep the fence on the left and woodland on the right to reach a stile. Beyond, there is a choice of paths: the lower is more pleasant as it hugs the shoreline to the end of the pool. Go across a car park to a stile by a gate (ignore the bridleway just before this).

Turn sharp right and head for a stile to the left of a gateway. Go over and head uphill towards a gate to the left of a clump of trees. Cross the field beyond, passing to the right of a fenced ditch to a stile by red-brick terraced houses (seen end on). Go over two stiles to a lane in **Shuttington**.

Go up the lane opposite, passing the church. Now ignore a gate on the left, going through a gate at the rear of the churchyard on to a gravel path and following it to a lane. Do not turn left: instead, go right up the easily missed alleyway behind the fence on the other side of the drive. Go over a stile at the end, turn left over another stile and then straight ahead, over another stile. Keep the hedgerow on your left over two more stiles on to a lane. Turn right to a T-junction. Turn left to go under the M42, and turn right at the first junction. Cross a railway bridge into **Polesworth** and watch for a left turn into High Street, with an old Pauper's School on the corner. A short way along on the right, walk under the 15th-century Abbey Gatehouse to reach the church. Opposite the door, take the alleyway signed to the village and turn left to Abbey Green. Cross a footbridge over the river Anker, turn right over the busy junction and go up Tamworth Road (Fire Station on the corner) to rejoin the Coventry Canal. Turn right along the towpath for 2 miles to return to Bridge 59, passing the **Alvecote Pools** Nature Reserve along the way.

POINTS OF INTEREST:

Alvecote Priory – A small Benedictine priory, established as a cell to Great Malvern by William Burdet in 1159. Little remains except a moulded doorway from the late 14th century and a stone dovecote. The site is now a peaceful picnic area.

Shuttington – The Norman church of St Matthew was once a chapel to Alvecote Priory. Buried here is Thomas Spooner who, at 40 stones, was the fattest man in England in the 18th century.

Polesworth – St Editha's Abbey Church, founded in 827 and dedicated to King Alfred's daughter, once served a Benedictine nunnery.

Alvecote Pools – The Nature Reserve is owned by British Coal and managed by the Warwickshire Wildlife Trust. Mining subsidence created the pools and after the colliery closed in 1965, nature (with a little help) took over and the spoil heaps were slowly reclaimed. The site has been an SSSI since 1955 and is superb for wetland birds as well as supporting a rich and varied flora. Recorded birds include Great-crested Grebe, Pochard, Tufted Duck, Snipe, Redshank and Little Ringed Plover.

REFRESHMENTS:

The Wolferstan Arms, Shuttington.
The Bull's Head, Polesworth.

Walk 83 LONG COMPTON AND ROLLRIGHT STONES 8m (13km)

Maps: OS Sheets Landranger 151; Pathfinder 1044.

Following farm tracks and minor roads to ancient stone circle.
Marvellous views.

Start: At 287331, Long Compton Church.

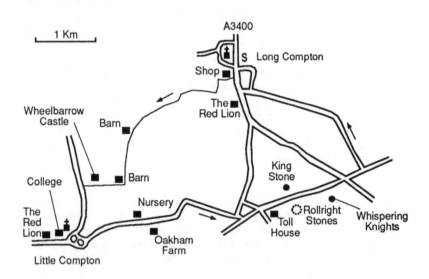

Please show consideration to local residents as there is limited parking in Long Compton.

Start the walk from the church and walk southwards, with care, along the A3400, passing shops to reach the old village pump (housed in the base of an old cross). Turn right through a metal gate, go down a farm drive and through another gate. Follow the drive along the edge of a field, then swing left to go through another gate. Keep on the well-defined farm lane beyond, going through numerous gates, for over a mile passing to the left of a barn complex. Go through a gateway and climb uphill, with woods on the right. From here, wonderful views open out behind you towards **Long Compton**. Go through a gateway and walk up on to the plateau ahead. Just beyond the barns in front is a junction of paths: turn right along the right edge of the next two fields,

158

passing a house (Wheelbarrow Castle) and a barn to reach a minor road. Turn left down the hill into **Little Compton**. Keep right at a junction, passing the church to reach a T-junction. Turn left – the Red Lion lies down the road to the right. Follow the road around the outskirts of the village, climbing up the minor road on to the ridge, with views stretching across the Cotswolds and into Oxfordshire. Go past a nursery and Oakham Farm, then swing left, and then right, by a quarry. Unfortunately, paths on the map which appear to offer short cuts on this road section are unmarked and ill-defined on the ground, so follow the road, ignoring a left turn, to a T-junction. Turn left to go over a crossroads by an old toll house and go straight on, along the road, which also runs along the county boundary, to reach the **Rollright Stones**.

The main circle is on the right (with a reasonable entrance fee, donated to animal charities); the King Stone monolith stands in a field opposite; and the Whispering Knights are in a field further down the road on the right. Stay on the road to its junction with the A3400 and cross, with care, to a lane opposite. After $\frac{1}{4}$ mile, turn left down a minor road to return to Long Compton.

POINTS OF INTEREST:

Long Compton – The murder of an old woman in 1875 by Jems Heywood sparked a tradition of witchcraft. He claimed she was a witch who had cast an evil eye on his livestock. The mostly 13th-century Church of St Peter and St Paul has a charming 400 year old, two storey lychgate.

Little Compton – This quiet village has a 17th-century manor house, the former home of Bishop Juxon, which is now a business college. Bishop Juxon, who attended Charles I at his execution, became the Archbishop of Canterbury and officiated at the Coronation of Charles II. The beautiful Church of St Denys has a 14th-century saddleback tower and a stained glass window showing the story of Charles I's execution. Spot the mistake made by the stonemason (and the attempted correction) on the Leverton Harris tomb.

Rollright Stones – The remarkable Bronze Age stone circle known as the King's Men is 100 feet in diameter and dates from around 1500 BC, though its origins and purpose remain a mystery. The Whispering Knights are the remains of a burial chamber. The stones stand on an early trackway, the Jurassic Way, which ran from the shores of the Humber to Salisbury Plain and the south coast.

REFRESHMENTS:
The Red Lion, Long Compton.
The Red Lion, Little Compton.

Walk 84   ALCESTER AND COUGHTON COURT   8m (13km)

Maps: OS Sheets Landranger 150; Pathfinder 997 and 975.

A pleasant river and stream-side ramble, passing a National Trust Manor.

Start: At 091577, School Road car park, Alcester.

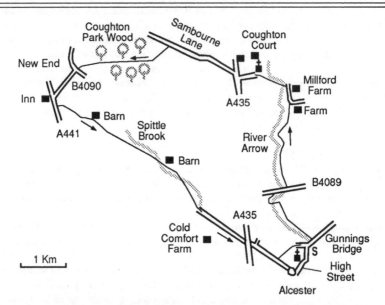

There is ample parking in **Alcester** but the walk starts in School Road. Turn left over Gunnings Bridge and left again by Greig Sports Hall, passing two football fields. Numerous paths wind among the trees, but keep the River Arrow on your left to reach an old railway line. Turn left, over the river and right, with the river on the right, to a bridge. Climb up to the B4089, turn right over a bridge and then go left to rejoin the riverside path, the river again being on your left. The path hugs the riverside through several fields and, after a mile, reaches a stile beside a gate, by farm buildings. Go over and turn left along a lane, passing Millford Farm. Turn left over a footbridge and cross a field to a handgate. Go half-right, towards the church, to reach a gate on to a lane. Turn left to a junction with the A435 junction. The entrance to **Coughton Court** is along on the right.

Turn right, with care, then left down Sambourne Lane. Go over an old railway bridge and, just before Coughton Park Wood, take the bridleway on the left, by four wooden posts. Follow the bridleway, swinging right into the wood. Stay on the broad path through the wood, then head across a field to reach a gate on to a road. Cross the busy junction with care, then go uphill along the B4090 to its junction with the A441 at New End. Turn left, with care, and just past the inn, go over an awkward stile on the left. Cross to the stile ahead and go through the scrub beyond. Climb another stile and walk half-right to a stile into a wood. Drop down to another stile and, in the next field, descend through a line of trees, passing a barn to reach a gate in the far left corner. Turn right down a lane and cross to a stile opposite, by a barn.

Keep a hedge on your right to join a path beside Spittle Brook. Keep the brook on your left across several large fields. Ignore the first gap, but cross the Brook at the next, by a ruined barn. Turn right and, shortly, recross the Brook. Now turn left with the Brook again on your left. At the end of the next field, recross the Brook and turn right, (the Brook is now on your right). Go through several hedge gaps, until the path again crosses the Brook. Turn left and, at the end, swing right to a farm lane. Turn left, and left again over a bridge by the drive to Cold Comfort Farm. The lane crosses a bridge over the A435 to reach Allimore Road. Keep ahead, going over an old railway bridge and across at a junction into Seggs Lane. Go straight over the roundabout towards the High Street. The start is at the top end, beyond the church.

POINTS OF INTEREST:

Alcester – This was originally a Roman settlement on Icknield Street, becoming a free borough in the reign of Henry I. Granted a weekly market and annual fair in the late 13th century, it became the centre of a thriving linen manufacturing industry. Later industries included the making of gloves, nails, guns, needles and malt. The old malt house is the oldest house in the town, dating from about 1500. St Nicholas' Church has a 14th-century tower crowned by pinnacles. The east end was rebuilt following a fire in the 18th century.

Coughton Court – For nearly 600 years the home of the Throckmorton family and, since 1945, in the care of the National Trust. The Court houses fine collections of furniture and paintings and the chemise worn by Mary, Queen of Scots, at her execution. St Peter's Church was built in the 15th century by Sir Robert Throckmorton.

REFRESHMENTS:

The Nevill Arms, New End.
There is a tea shop at Coughton Court when it is open.
There is also plenty of choice in Alcester.

Walk 85   ASTON CANTLOW AND KINWARTON   8m (13km)

Maps: OS Sheets Landranger 150 and 151; Pathfinder 997.

An enjoyable ramble, full of interest. Some paths are ill-defined.

Start: At138598, Aston Cantlow Church.

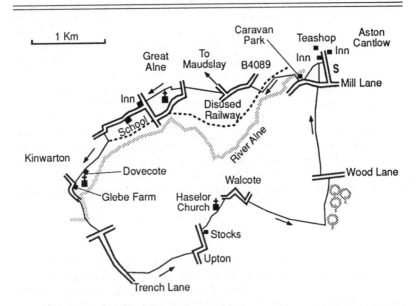

Parking is limited in Aston Cantlow so please show consideration to residents: the inn car park is for patrons only. Alternative parking is available in the lay-by near Great Alne Church.

From **Aston Cantlow** churchyard, take the right-hand of two signed paths, going through the churchyard to reach a path to Mill Lane. Turn right, along the path to the left of the caravan park entrance. Follow the waymarkers across the footbridge, then bear left beside the River Alne to reach a double stile and footbridge. The dismantled railway to the right was built in 1876. Cross the bridge and walk to the top right corner to reach an enclosed path. Follow this to a lane and turn right. Turn left along the B4089 and take the second turning on the right, signed to Maudslay. Now turn right along the path to the left of the notices, and head for a protruding fence corner. Go past a cricket field and the rear of gardens, then cross a lane to an alleyway that

162

leads to the church in Great Alne. A sign warns that there is no footpath through the churchyard, so turn right, over a stile, and go left beside the churchyard. Now follow field edges to emerge opposite the inn. Turn left, then right along the B4089, passing the school. After a sharp left bend, go through the right-hand of two gates on the left. Follow the hedge on the left through a gate and aim half-right, passing the dovecote in **Kinwarton**.

Go past the church and farm, and where the lane turns right, swing left along a No Through Road. At its end, cross a field to a footbridge and go up the lane beyond to a T-junction. Turn right, and immediately left up Trench Lane. After about $\frac{1}{2}$ mile watch for a marker on the left by a metal gate. The field beyond has no headland and can be tough going in summer. Follow the hedge on the right across two fields to reach a gap on the right, then go left to reach a lane in Upton. Go through the village and turn right by the village stocks. The tarmac path leads past **Haselor** Church to Walcote. Keep ahead along the road, swinging right, then at the next left bend, cross the stile ahead down a lane. Follow the hedge on the right across three fields, the path switching sides in the fourth field. At the edge of woodland, turn left along a bridleway to reach a gate on to Wood Lane. Turn left and, shortly, right over a hidden fence stile. Follow the hedge on the left to join a farm track to Mill Lane. The footpath opposite heads across two fields to the churchyard in Aston Cantlow.

POINTS OF INTEREST:
Aston Cantlow – The village name comes from the Cantilupe family who built the castle in the early 12th century. Only a few earthworks remain. In 1227 the village was granted a weekly market and annual fair but a similar grant to, and the subsequent prospering of, nearby Henley-in-Arden prevented Aston Cantlow developing in the same way. The marriage of Mary Arden to John Shakespeare was solemnised in St John the Baptist's Church.
Kinwarton – The tiny St Mary's Church was rebuilt in 1316. Inside can be seen an alabaster table dedicated to the Madonna and an ancient oak framed window. The 14th-century dovecote, now in the care of the National Trust, was given to the Abbey of Evesham by King Cenred of Mercia in 708. In the days when enough fresh meat could not be kept through the winter, the birds provided a useful supplement.
Haselor – St Mary and All Saints' Church has a small Norman tower and a chancel with Jacobean panelling.

REFRESHMENTS:
The King's Head, Aston Cantlow.
Mother Huff Cap Inn, Great Alne.

Walk 86   **FILLONGLEY**   8m (13km)
Maps: OS Sheets Landranger 140; Pathfinder 935.
An enjoyable, undulating walk past castle earthworks, across
fields and passing Fillongley Hall.
Start: At 281873, north of the crossroads in Fillongley.

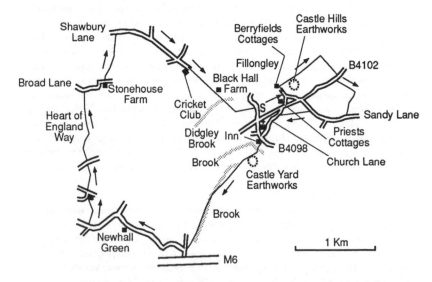

Walk to the crossroads, turn left down the B4102, and go left along Berryfields, passing
the Priests Cottages. Built in 1893 they are the homes of retired preachers. Look for
the earthworks of Castle Hills over to the right, then follow the signs through the
buildings of Berryfields Farm. Go along a field edge and over a stile, then, shortly,
turn right and go through a spinney. Go over a footbridge and turn left along a field
edge. At the field end, turn right up a track to the B4102. Turn right and, shortly, left
over a stile. Follow the hedge on the right across two fields, then turn right along a
field edge to reach Sandy Lane. Turn right for $1/_2$ mile, then go left along a path over
rough ground. Continue along the path as it crosses fields to reach the recreation
ground. Turn left down Church Lane to its T-junction with the B4098. To shorten the
walk, turn right here to return to the crossroads.

Turn left, past the inn and the newsagents, then right along a path, signed 'Country Walk'. This well-marked path leads right, over a brook, and to the right of the castle earthworks. Follow the fence on the left to a stile by a holly bush. Go over and half-left, crossing a brook via stepping stones and going ahead to cross another stile. Follow the hedge on the right across several fields, eventually walking beside a brook. Join a wide track, cross a field and go along an old road to the B4102. Go down the road opposite, through Newhall Green, and bear left at a junction. Now, after several hundred yards, take the Heart of England Way (*see* Note to Walk 66) on the right. Go half-left across a field, over a stile and aim for the houses ahead to reach a lane. Turn right to reach a junction, and take the path opposite, passing a farm. Aim for the top right corner of a field, cross a lane and the stile opposite and head straight across the field beyond. Go over a stile and aim for the top right corner to reach another stile. Follow the hedge on the left, then turn left over a stile and walk through a copse. Cross a field towards a power pole, go over a stile and follow the hedge on the right to a corner. Head straight across the field beyond to a stile by a protruding hedge corner. Go over and turn right along Broad Lane, leaving the Heart of England Way.

Go past Stonehouse Farm and, just past the bend, turn left over a stile. Follow the hedge on the right across several fields to reach Shawbury Lane. Turn right, go over the junction with Broad lane (ignoring a stile on the left) and, shortly, turn right over a stile. Cross the Cricket Club entrance and walk diagonally across waymarked fields to pass to the right of Black Hall Farm. Follow the hedge on the left, cross Didgley Brook and several fields to reach a double stile. Go over, turn left and follow the hedge on the left to emerge into **Fillongley**.

POINTS OF INTEREST:

Fillongley – Only ridges and furrows show the sites of two castles. The 12th-century earthworks of Castle Hills was possibly abandoned by the time of Henry III. The slightly later Castle Yard site was refortified by the Hastings family. The 13th-century St Mary and All Saints' Church has medieval stained glass in the nave windows. Extended in the 16th century, further restoration work was carried out in 1887. The area has associations with George Eliot: nearby Arbury Park was her birthplace and her uncle, Isaac Peatson, is buried in the churchyard. Fillongley Hall, the family seat of Lord Norton, dates back to 1840. George Eliot stayed at Bede Cottage on the estate and it is believed that this provided the inspiration for her novel, Adam Bede.

REFRESHMENTS:
The Butcher's Arms, Fillongley.
The Manor House, Fillongley.

Walk 87   **MIDDLETON**   8m (13km)

Maps: OS Sheets Landranger 139; Pathfinder 913 and 914.

A Nature Reserve, a canal, a charming village and a stately home feature on this superb walk.

Start: At 205970, Broomey Croft car park, Kingsbury Water Park.

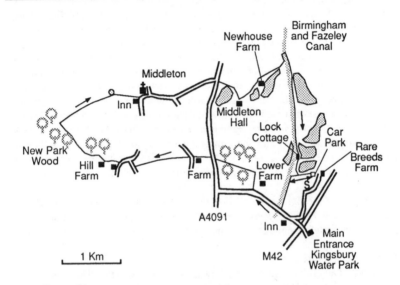

The car park is accessible not via the main entrance to Kingsbury Water Park (*see* Note to Walk 33) but down a lane just after the M42 and before the canal.

With your back to the lake, go to the top right corner of the car park to reach a lane. Turn right, walk over another track, through a wooden barrier and go right down the lane to join the Birmingham and Fazeley Canal towpath. Turn left, passing a lock. At the next bridge, turn right down the road past Lower Farm and take a path on the right. Follow the hedge on the left and, at the end of the field, turn left straight across the field and the drive to the Hall. Follow the path ahead, between poplar trees, and cross the next field to reach a gate onto the busy A4091. Cross, with great care, turn right and immediately left along a path by a sub-station. Follow the hedges on the left, passing Hunts Green Farm to reach a lane. Turn right and immediately left into a

166

field. Follow the hedge on the left across several fields, going under power lines. Then, when the hedge ends, continue ahead across a field to reach Green Lane. Turn right past Corner House, and then left at a T-junction.

Turn right before a house to go down a farm track. Veer right past the buildings of Hill Farm and go through a gate. Go downhill, swinging left with the track past Aldermore Spinney, and cross a footbridge over Langley Brook. Head for the right-hand corner of New Park Wood and take the path through the edge of the woods. Part of the woods is used for clay pigeon shooting so proceed with caution and if shooting is in progress, make sure the marshals are aware of your approach. After nearly $^{1}/_{2}$ mile, by a pool, turn right along a path that crosses fields and a shooting range. Follow the hedge on the right over several fields, aiming towards **Middleton** church. Go past a pool to join a vehicle track and bear right into Church Lane. Walk past the school and church and cross the busy A4091 with care. Go down the drive opposite, passing a lake to reach **Middleton Hall**. Follow the drive to the left, before the Hall, going left again in front of Newhouse Farm. Go through a gate and along a bridleway beside trees. Turn left, go over a stream and follow the canal to cross a bridge. Turn right down the canal towpath for a mile, leaving the water just before Lock Cottage. Turn right (with lakes on the left) to reach the car park.

POINTS OF INTEREST:
Middleton Hall – A mix of Elizabethan, Jacobean and Georgian styles, from the 15th century. This was the 18th-century home of Sir Francis Willoughby. Now a conservation centre restored by a charitable trust, it houses a craft centre. The man-made lake in the grounds, now an SSSI, was inspired by John Ray, a naturalist who stayed at the Hall in the 17th century. The deer park was lost to modern gravel workings. The Hall is open from April to October on Sundays and Bank Holidays in the afternoons only.
Middleton – St John the Baptist Church, begun in the 12th century, is built of sandstone and has a Norman south doorway and monuments to the Willoughby family. Inside are the gauntlet and gloves of a man whose skeleton was found in the moat. His bones, and those of the horse found with him, are buried in the churchyard.

There is a rare breeds farm close to the car park entrance which is open from April to October.

REFRESHMENTS:
The Green Man, Middleton.
The Dog and Doublet, near the canal.
There is a coffee shop at Middleton Hall.

Walk 88   LEAMINGTON AND OFFCHURCH   8m (13km)

Maps: OS Sheets Landranger 151; Pathfinder 976.

A walk across parkland to an attractive village, returning along a canal and through colourful gardens.

Start: 334657, Newbold Comyn Country Park.

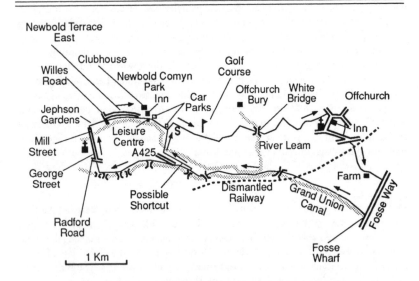

Start from the furthest car park, by the children's adventure playground. Take the path at the top left corner of the car park. Turn right along a wide path between hedges, with a golf course on the left. The path swings right, then left around the end of the course. Go right along a footpath hidden in bushes. Cross a field, and in the next field follow the hedge on the left. (To cross Offchurch Bury Park, the footpath follows the course used in cross country riding events, so please be alert for thundering hooves!) Go over a stile and bear right to cross the River Leam via White Bridge. Turn right through trees, cross a bridge and stile, then turn right beside a field, swinging left at its end to walk with a ditch on your right. At the second drive, turn right and follow the road to a slight bend, where the path turns left towards trees. Turn right, with the trees on your left, to reach a stile in the corner. Now leave the course, heading straight across a sloping field, then bearing right to a stile by a gate.

Turn right into **Offchurch**, passing the inn. (The first road on the right leads to the church.) Ignore the Hunningham road on the left, going over a stile on the right. Follow the hedge on the right, walking uphill to a road. Turn left and, at the main road junction, cross, with care, to the stile opposite. Head downhill, crossing a dismantled railway and bearing half-right across the field beyond to reach a track beside the fence. Go left of farm buildings, uphill and across a field to reach the Fosse Way. Turn right, with care, along this fast and dangerous road to reach Fosse Wharf on the Grand Union Canal (*see* Note to Walk 5). Turn right and follow the towpath for nearly 3 miles. (At Bridge 36, it is possible to shorten the walk to 6 miles by turning left up the A425 to a car park on the right. Cross the footbridge and bear half left to the Country Park.) Leave the canal at the 10th bridge, by Flavels factory, turning right up an alleyway and going under the railway to reach Radford Road in **Leamington**. Turn left, then right along George Street. Go ahead into Mill Street and, at its end, cross the suspension bridge into Jephson Gardens. Turn right through the gardens to Willes Road. Turn left, then right up Newbold Terrace East. Now go along the grass to return to Newbold Comyn Country Park.

POINTS OF INTEREST:
Offchurch – Offa, the Saxon King of Mercia, had associations with the village. He built a palace on the site now occupied by Offchurch Bury House and founded St Gregory's Church. Two carved stones in the chancel wall are possibly part of the Kings' coffin lid and his son is also reputedly buried here. Excavations on the site of the church in 1866 revealed an ancient burial ground containing weapons and jewellery dating to 650AD.
Leamington Spa – This beautiful town is well known as a spa resort and has fine examples of Regency architecture. In 1786 William Abbots built the first spa baths: the Pump Room was constructed in 1814 by Henry Jephson and visited by the Prince Regent in 1819. The Jephson Memorial in the gardens was erected in 1849 to commemorate Dr Henry Jephson who treated his patients with the spa waters and helped put the town on the map. All Saints' Church dates from 1086, its 145 foot tower being added at the turn of the century. Inside there are matchstick models of the church and Coventry Cathedral.

REFRESHMENTS:
Newbold Comyn Arms, in the Country Park.
The Stag's Head, Offchurch.
There is also plus plenty of choice in Leamington.

Walk 89   STOURBRIDGE CANAL AND FENS POOL   8m (13km)

Maps: OS Sheets Landranger 139; Pathfinder 933. The Birmingham A-Z is also useful.

A walk from a Nature Reserve along canals threading a way through the Black Country.

Start: At 913885, the Nature Reserve car park.

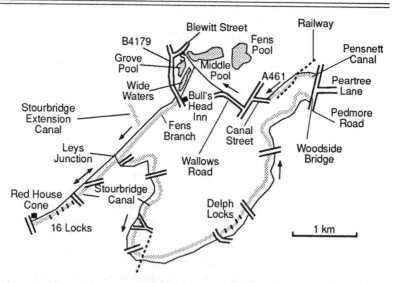

Although this walk is not through the prettiest countryside in the area, there is plenty of canal history on view, plus wildlife to be seen at the Nature Reserve. The car park is off Blewitt Street, off the B4179.

Go down the right-hand of the two main paths, then follow the stony path by Grove Pool. The path descends, then bears right beside Wide Waters to reach the B4179 by the Bull's Head. Cross the road to reach the towpath of the Fens Branch Canal. Follow the towpath past the Stourbridge Extension Canal which was opened in 1840 to link the local industries to the canal network. When you reach Leys Junction, a detour of 2 miles follows the towpath past Stourbridge 16 Locks to reach the Red House Cone. This unique building was constructed in 1790 and originally produced window glass, later producing tableware and crystal. It is now a glass museum.

170

Return to Leys Junction, crossing the canal at Stourbridge Top Lock to join the towpath of the **Stourbridge Canal**. Follow the towpath past Delph locks, through an area known as the Waterfront, and along the outskirts of Brierley Hill. Go under Woodside Bridge, then leave the canal, turning right along Pedmore Road and crossing Peartee Lane.

Cross Pedmore road and take a path on the left towards a works. Turn right along a path beside the Pensnett Canal. After a short distance this path goes under a freight railway line and then joins Canal Street. Follow this to its T-junction with the A461. Turn left, then cross, with care, and, shortly, turn right down Wallows Road. Keep ahead where the road swings left, going along a path which leads back into the **Nature Reserve**. Stay on the main path which leads back to the car park.

POINTS OF INTEREST:

Stourbridge Canal – The canal was opened in 1779 and linked the Staffordshire and Worcestershire Canal with the Dudley Canal. Stourbridge Flight is a set of 16 locks which stretches for a mile. Delph Locks are an impressive flight, rebuilt in 1850. They are known as the Nine Locks, although there are only eight. The remains of the originals can be seen alongside the current flight.

Buckpool and Fens Pool Nature Reserve – The Reserve is a valuable habitat of pools, grassland and scrub deep in the Black Country and surrounded by housing. One hundred years ago, the area was at the heart of working collieries, claypits, brick, iron and steel works. Most of the works had closed by the early 1900's and over the years nature has transformed the area, although some scars are still visible today. The pools are still used as top-up reservoirs for the canal system. They also provide a safe haven for wintering and migrant birds. The pools are one of the few urban wetlands to nurture rare amphibians such as the smooth and great crested newt, as well as the more common frogs and toads. Various species of dragonflies are also present in significant numbers. All manner of wildflowers, including significant number of southern marsh orchids, thrive. Wide Waters, at the end of the Fens branch of the canal, is the site of old wharves where the iron and coal were loaded from the railway to barges to be transported. Excellent informative leaflets on this area, and all the other pockets of countryside in the Black Country, are available from Dudley Council – tel: 01384 453522 for details.

REFRESHMENTS:

The Bull's Head, on the B4179 by the canal.
The Samson and Lion, by Stourbridge Locks.

Walk 90 **ULLENHALL** 8m (13km)

Maps: OS Sheets Landranger 139 and 150; Pathfinder 975.

A pleasant walk across pastoral landscape to a beautiful bluebell wood.

Start: At 122673, Ullenhall Church.

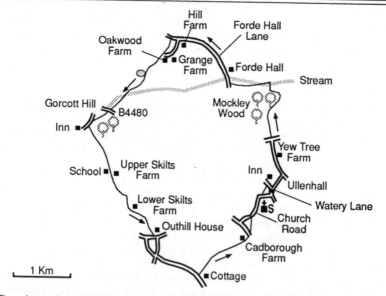

There is ample roadside parking by the church, but please be considerate, and do not expect space when services are being held.

From the church, take the path opposite across pasture to emerge between houses into **Ullenhall**, opposite the inn. Turn right along the lane, then take the first left turning. Go left again at the junction and walk along Watery Lane to reach a T-junction. Turn left along the lane, passing Yew Tree Farm to reach another T-junction. Take the footpath opposite, walking straight across a field. Go through a gate and follow the hedge on the right to a gate into Mockley Wood. Now follow the markers along the edge, then go through the wood and over a stile at its end into a field. Walk ahead, going over a brook then turning left to reach the end of the field, with the wood on your left. Cross stiles, following the hedge on the right to reach Forde Hall Lane.

Turn right along the lane, passing Forde Hall. Just past Hill Farm, turn left on a bridleway along the lane to reach Grange Farm. Follow the track through Oakwood Farm, going through two gates, then take a path on the left, leaving the bridleway. Cross a field to its far right corner, then maintain direction to pass a pool and go over a stile. Continue to reach a metal gate. Go through and maintain direction across the next two fields, going over a stile and brook in the far corner of the second. Now head towards the cottages in the distance to reach the B4480. Cross, with care, and take the path opposite, following the fence and wood on the left to reach a stile. Go over and turn left along a lane in Gorcott Hill. Shortly, turn left again down a school drive. Go past the school and Upper Skilts Farm and walk along a broad farm track for over a mile.

At the track's junction with a concrete track, bear left along the lane past Lower Skilts Farm. Follow the hedge on the left in the next field to reach a stile by a pool. Go over and follow the left field edge, keeping right of the farm. Go over a stile and down the drive to reach a road. Turn left and, shortly, right down a lane to reach a crossroads. Turn left and, after nearly a mile, by a cottage, take a path on the left. Follow the hedge on the right to reach a stile. Go over and follow the hedge on the left to reach a gate in the far corner. Now follow the fence on the right, going through a gate and walking beside a wood (on your right) to reach another gate. Go through and follow the hedge on the left, passing Cadborough Farm to reach a road. Turn left, cross and, shortly, take a faint path on the right. Go through bushes, over a stile and across a meadow. Walk half-left across the field beyond to reach a stile on to a lane. Turn right along Church Road to return to the church in **Ullenhall**.

POINTS OF INTEREST:

Ullenhall – The Knight family have been associated with Ullenhall since 1554: Robert Knight was granted the title of Earl of Catherlow, Viscount Barrells of Barrells Park. The coat of arms of the family was a winged spur, hence the name of the village inn. The Church of St Mary the Virgin dates from the 19th century. The ruins of the old church lie across fields to the east of the village.

REFRESHMENTS:

The Winged Spur, Ullenhall.
The Holly Bush Inn, Gorcott Hill.

Walk 91   **WAST HILLS AND WEATHEROAK** $8\frac{1}{2}$m ($13\frac{1}{2}$km)

Maps: OS Sheets Landranger 139; Pathfinder 954.

Enjoyable walking around quiet hills, south of Birmingham. Well waymarked.

Start: At 055756, Forhill picnic area.

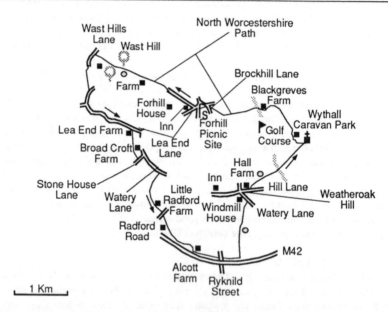

Take the North Worcestershire Path (*see* Note to Walk 64) to the right of the toilets, cross the road, go past the inn and down Lea End Lane. Shortly, turn right down the road signed to Forhill House. Continue almost to the end, then turn right over a stile and left through pasture to skirt a farm. Go past a pond, over a stile and keep the hedge on your right across three fields. Ignore a stile on the right, crossing the stile ahead to join a tarmac track. Go through trees, veer right in front of gates and keep a hedge on your left across two fields (the canal is under your feet in a tunnel). Turn left down Wast Hills Lane and watch for a path on the right running parallel to the lane and emerging lower down. Turn right and, at a T-junction, turn left along Lea End Lane.

Just after Lea End Farm, turn right on to a path around the farm and then head south across fields. Pass Broadcroft Farm, on the left, to reach Stonehouse Lane. Turn left to a T-junction. Turn right into Watery Lane and, after $\frac{1}{2}$ mile, go over a stile on the right, by a gate. Keep the hedge on your left, going over stiles, and at its end swing south towards fish ponds. Skirt Little Radford Farm, cross two stiles and a bridleway, and then walk with a hedge on your left. Now go straight across the next field to reach Radford Road. Turn right and, shortly, left down a farm track, passing a house and Alcott Farm to reach the M42. Walk parallel to the motorway, going over several stiles. Cross Ryknild Street and continue over two fields to reach a field corner where the path goes left. Keep the hedge on your right across six fields, passing a pond and aiming for the grounds of Windmill House. Go over a stile by a gate and continue to Watery Lane. Turn left to the crossroads on **Weatheroak Hill** – the inn is downhill on the left.

Turn right up Hill Lane and, just past Hall Farm, go over a stile on the left, by a gate, and follow a footpath to another stile. Go over, cross the field beyond, pass a pond and, keeping the hedge on your left, continue to a footbridge over a stream. Cross and head north-east across fields to reach **Wythall**. After visiting the church, return to the path junction and swing right, skirting a caravan park. Cross a stile and follow the right edge of a golf course. Now swing left and turn right over a ditch and a stile. Negotiate a small paddock, climb a stile by buildings and skirt Blackgreves Farm. Cross a bridge over a stream and follow the hedge on your right (you are back on the North Worcestershire Path) across two fields, ignoring paths going left to reach Brockhill Lane. Turn right and, shortly, left to return to the picnic site.

POINTS OF INTEREST:

Weatheroak Hill – The Hill is crossed by Icknield Street, an old Roman road. The 17th-century Blackgreves Farm is surrounded on all sides by a moat. According to legend, a Roman soldier drowned in the moat in 47AD. Weatheroak Hall dates from the 18th century and was almost completely rebuilt in 1884. It was once the home of the Mynors family and is now used as the golf clubhouse.

Wythall – St Mary's Church was built in 1862. The huge red and blue brick tower was paid for, in 1908, by the Mynors family in memory of their parents.

REFRESHMENTS:

The Peacock Inn, Forhill.
The Coach and Horses, Weatheroak.

Walk 92   COLESHILL AND MAXSTOKE   8½m (13½km)

Maps: OS Sheets Landranger 139; Pathfinder 935 and 914.

A marvellous walk full of interest, past an ancient castle and priory.

Start: At 201891, Church Hill, Coleshill.

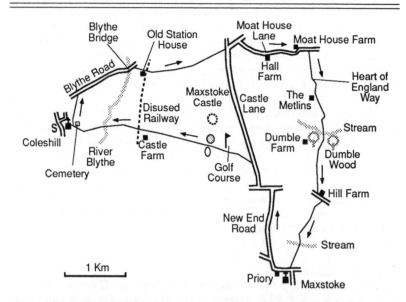

There is ample parking in **Coleshill**, but the walk starts on Church Hill. Pass right of the church, then go half-left across the green (signed 'Country Walk'). Turn left through the cemetery on to an enclosed path. Go through a paddock and past a field, then turn left down a drive. Turn right along the B4114 to just beyond Blythe Bridge, then go over a stile on the right. Walk ahead, but shortly turn left, over a stile, and go along the right edge of a field. Cross two stiles, by a house, and the line of the old Whitacre to Hampton in Arden railway. Walk along the right edge of the field beyond, passing a redundant stile and bearing half-left towards the far hedge and a line of pylons. Follow the hedge on the left to reach a lane at a crossroads. Cross, then turn right down Moat House Lane, passing Moat House Farm. Now take the Heart of England Way (*see* Note to Walk 66), on the right.

Follow the marker posts across fields towards the pylon line, then beside trees to cross the drive to The Metlins. Follow the hedge on the right and, shortly, bear left across a field, going downhill to Dumble Wood. Follow the markers through the wood and go over a bridge. Now leave the Heart of England Way, following the hedge on the left to reach a road by Hill Farm. Turn left, past the farm, and, shortly, take a path on the right. Turn right along a field edge, go over a ditch and along a field edge to a gate. Go through and half-right across the next field to its top right corner. Follow the hedge on the right over a ditch and across fields to **Maxstoke**.

Turn right past the church and priory, and follow the road, ignoring a left fork to reach a T-junction. Turn left and, shortly, right down Castle Lane. Join a footpath on the left and follow the hedge on the right (ignoring a stile on the right) to reach a stile on to a golf course. Head straight over the course, with **Maxstoke Castle** to the right. Go between pools and follow the fence on the left to a stile. Walk through Birch Wood and along a wide track past Castle Farm and the old railway. Keep ahead when the track bends right, and go over the River Blythe into a field. Follow a wide track uphill, go over a stile and bear right to a kissing gate. Turn left, then right into the cemetery. Now go left to rejoin the outward path, reversing it to the start.

POINTS OF INTEREST:

Coleshill – The Norman 14th-century Church of St Peter and St Paul contains a beautiful 12th-century font decorated with sculptured figures. Simon Digby inherited the manor and lands of Coleshill from the de Montforts and the church houses many tombs of the Digby family.

Maxstoke – The ruins of the courtyard, church tower, granary, gatehouses and Prior's lodgings are all that remain of an Augustine Priory founded in 1342 by William de Clinton. The Priory was dissolved in 1538 and granted to Charles Brandon, Duke of Suffolk. It is now privately owned and not open to the public. St Michael's Church was built around 1340. On the floor of the sanctuary are 14th-century tiles excavated from the ruins of the priory.

Maxstoke Castle – Built by William de Clinton, Earl of Huntingdon, in the 1340's, this was a fortified moated house rather than a castle. It was later held by the Duke of Buckingham, who helped Richard III to gain the throne. Buckingham was executed by Richard when he backed Henry Tudor's (later Henry VII) attempt to seize the crown. The castle passed to Sir Thomas Dilke in 1589, his descendants still owning it. Although not open to the public, it has occasional open days in aid of local charities.

REFRESHMENTS:

There is plenty of choice in Coleshill.

Walk 93   KNOWLE AND TEMPLE BALSALL   9m (14$\frac{1}{2}$km)

Maps: OS Sheets Landranger 139; Pathfinder 954 and 955.

A fascinating walk, visiting ancient almshouses, several churches and a canal.

Start: At 183767, High Street, Knowle.

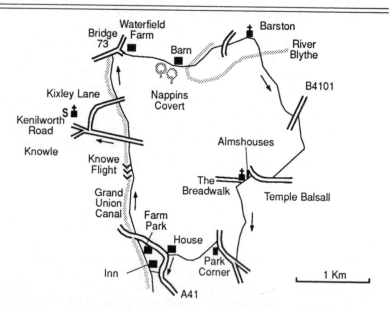

Walk up Kenilworth Road, past the church, and turn left up Kixley Lane to the Grand Union Canal. Turn left (northwards) up the canal as far as the second bridge (No. 73). Turn right along a minor road, and right again up the drive to Waterfield Farm. Go through double gates between buildings and along a grassy lane past Nappins Covert. Go past a ruined barn and through a gateway, then turn left and go over a stile in the corner. Cross the field diagonally to reach a stile and cross pasture beyond to reach a footbridge over the River Blythe. Cross and go half-left to a stile. Climb the stile opposite and walk up a field to reach a stile between two trees. Walk past a house and barn, on the left, to reach a stile, also on the left, into **Barston** churchyard.

Turn right along the edge of the churchyard to reach a stile in the corner. Ignore a path going left and go ahead, through a hedgerow and over a stile. Walk with a hedge on your right, go through a gap and slightly left to cross the River Blythe. Turn right and follow a field boundary for about 300 yards, until a faint path goes left across the open field. If the path is unclear, aim slightly left of the pylons and, on nearing the fence, head for a stile and gate in the right corner. Turn left and, before a lay-by, go right over a stile. Walk along a field edge to a corner, go over a stile and turn right along a field. Go through a gate and turn right into **Temple Balsall**.

Turn left along a signed path, the Breadwalk, passing the Almshouses and St Mary's Church. Go over a bridge to reach a junction of paths. Turn left, through a gate, and follow a path as it curves right, with a hedge on the left, across a long field. Climb a stile on to a minor road and turn right. Keep right at a junction to reach a house, Park Corner. The path goes between the house and garage, becoming enclosed and going through a kissing gate on to a farm track. Turn right and follow the track through a gate. Just before a house, turn left through a gate and go over a stile on to the A41. Turn left, with care, along the road and then right, up the drive of the Black Boy Inn. Behind the inn, turn right along the towpath of the Grand Union Canal passing a Farm Park. Follow the towpath past the five locks of Knowle Flight to reach a bridge and turn left along the road into **Knowle**.

POINTS OF INTEREST:

Barston – St Swithin's Church was erected in 1721 and remodelled in 1899.

Temple Balsall – The almshouses were originally a hospital, founded in 1678 by Lady Katherine Leveson, the grand-daughter of Robert Dudley, Earl of Leicester. The hamlet and manor were presented to the Knights Templar (formed in 1118 during the Crusades to protect pilgrims to the Holy Land) by Roger de Mowbray in 1146. The order was forcibly disbanded in the early 1300s and the land given to the Hospitallers, knights pledged to care for the sick and wounded. St Mary's Church dates from the 1280s: the east window shows a Templar knight in a white habit with a red cross and a Hospitaller with a white cross on a black habit.

Knowle – St John the Baptist, St Lawrence and St Anne's Church was built by Walter Cook in 1402 and contains the tomb of a gypsy king, Lawrence Boswell, and a row of sedilia (stone seats) stranded half-way up the chancel wall. The church floor was at a higher level until the 18th century when a processional subway under the church was removed, lowering the floor and leaving the sedilia marooned.

REFRESHMENTS:

The Black Boy Inn, Heronfield.
The Bull's Head, Barston.
There are also numerous possibilities in Knowle.

Walk 94   RUGBY AND ASHLAWN CUTTING   9m (14½km)

Maps: OS Sheets Landranger 140; Pathfinder 956.
An historic town, canal and a Nature Reserve.
Start: At 504752, Market Place, Rugby.

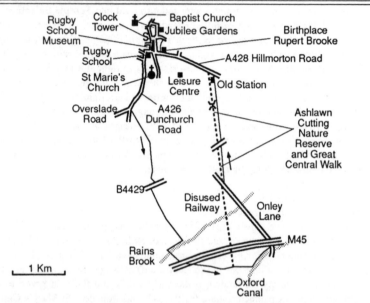

From the Clocktower in **Rugby,** go through the Market Place, turning right into Chapel Street. Turn left down Drury Lane, cross Lawrence Sheriff Street – Rugby School is to the left – and walk down Dunchurch Road (the A426), passing St Marie's Church, to the Overslade Road junction. Turn left along a bridleway. Go between hedges, over a road and along the right edge of a playing field. Go down the alleyway, across Ecton Leys, passing a cul-de-sac, and turn left through a gap in the hedge. Follow the hedge on the right and then a good headland across fields to cross the B4429.

Turn right and, shortly, left following the hedge on the left, then on the right, across two fields. Go through a gate and follow the fence on the right: the path is diverted and does not cross the field on the right. At the bottom of the field, turn right beside the field, then left along a track over Rains Brook. Follow the hedge on the right, then go left across a footbridge over the M45. At the far side, go left through a handgate: there are cattle in fields, so dogs must be on a lead. Cross the field, passing a dead tree to reach a waymarked gate in the top right corner. Head for the top right corner of the next field, passing through a thicket and going beneath an old railway bridge (ignore a footpath on the right). Cross the field ahead to reach a canal bridge.

Turn left along the Oxford Canal (*see* Note to Walk 8) towpath as far as the next bridge. Now turn left along Onley Lane and, just past the entrance to Lower Rainsbrook Farm, turn right through a gate on to the old Great Central Railway. Opened in 1899, this ran from London to Nottingham, finally closing in 1969. This stretch of the old line is part of the Great Central Walk from Newton village through **Ashlawn Cutting**. Follow the path under two bridges to reach the site of Hillmorton Station. Go under the next bridge, then up on to Hillmorton Road (the A428). Turn right, passing the leisure centre roundabout. Turn right along Church Walk, opposite Whitelaw House. On the corner is the birthplace of Rupert Brooke. More famous as a poet, he was also a housemaster at the school. Go down Church Walk, through the old parish churchyard and The Plaisance into Church Street. Turn left past St Andrew's Church, then turn right up Regent Street into Regent Place. Continue past the Baptist Church and Jubilee Gardens. Turn left at the top and left again into Chestnut Field. Turn left down North Street to return to the Market Place.

POINTS OF INTEREST:

Rugby – The famous public school was founded in 1567 on a site near the church, moving to its present position in 1750. The town's Tourist Office has details of school tours. The School Museum in Little Church Street and the James Gilbert Rugby Football Museum in Drury Street are also worth a visit. In Barby Road stands a statue of Thomas Hughes, famous as the author of *Tom Brown's Schooldays*, a semi-autobiographical account of his time as a pupil here. The tower of St Andrew's Church is believed to be built of stone taken from the old castle. The Town Trail leaflet – available from the Tourist Office – gives a comprehensive account of the town's fascinating history.

Ashlawn Cutting – The Nature Reserve is leased by the Warwickshire Wildlife Trust from Rugby Borough Council. The mixture of scrub and open grassy banks provides a rich habitat for wildlife. Plants colonising the banks include eyebright, cowslip, dwarf thistle, ox-eye daisy, and birds-foot trefoil. The blue fleabane is a county rarity. Butterflies, other insects and many birds also find a safe haven. The marshy areas are home to frogs, toads, newts and dragonflies.

REFRESHMENTS:

There is something to suit all tastes and pockets in Rugby.

181

Walk 95 HAY HEAD WOOD AND BARR BEACON 9¹/₂m (15km)

Maps: OS Sheets Landranger 139; Pathfinder 913.

A walk in remarkably unspoilt countryside, seemingly miles away from suburbia.

Start: At 033002, the car park at Park Lime Pits.

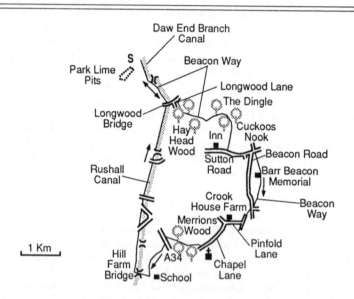

Park Lime Pits is reached at the end of Park Road, off Daw End Lane, Rushall. The walk follows the **Beacon Way** from the start to Rushall Canal and is well waymarked – despite the efforts of vandals to destroy the signposts! The Nature Reserves visited are in the care of Walsall Council. Leaflets are available – tel: 0121 360 9464.

At the entrance to the car park, join the towpath of the Daw End Branch Canal, walking south to the second bridge (Longwood). Cross the bridge and go over Longwood Lane to reach the open grassland which, between 1930 and 1960, was the site of Walsall airport.

Turn right past the car park and enter **Hay Head Wood** by the information board. Take the main path, to the left, following part of the nature trail, to reach the farthest end of the wood. Now follow an enclosed path beside fields to enter The Dingle, an area of mature beech and oak trees which was once a limestone quarry. Follow the waymarkers, bearing left on the main, very muddy, path along the right edge of the wood. A causeway and steps lead into Cuckoo's Nook, where the main path keeps near the left edge of the wood. Swing right at the end to reach the bottom corner of the wood, by a wooden board. Follow the hedge on the left across two fields to reach Sutton Road. Turn left along a path behind the bushes and cross the road at the waymarkers. Now turn left along the road. Cross Beacon Road at the lights and immediately turn right on to open grassland.

Walk left of the trees ahead and past the covered reservoirs to reach **Barr Beacon** memorial, built in the 1930's. Go through a car park and down a lane to Beacon Road. Cross to a path that is followed through a former quarry to reach a junction on Pinfold Lane. Go straight ahead, past Crook House Farm and down Chapel Lane. Just past St Margaret's Church, Great Barr, go through a gate on the right, walk along the avenue and go through Merrions Wood, bearing left to reach the A34. Cross, with care, and take the path ahead (still following the Beacon Way). Go over a bridge, then down the left side of school grounds. Turn sharp right to Hill Farm Bridge and then walk north along the towpath of the Rushall Canal for over 3 miles to join the outward path along the Daw End Branch Canal. Now reverse the outward route back to the start.

POINTS OF INTEREST:
Park Lime Pits – The pools were once a limestone quarry which supplied iron foundries via the canal system. Over 100 species of birds and 300 species of plants have been recorded in the Nature Reserve here.

Beacon Way – At 17 miles, the Way is one of the country's shortest long distance footpaths linking Chasewater Reservoir with Sandwell Valley Park. The Way uses existing rights of way along a green corridor of heath, woods, lakes and canal towpaths.

Hay Head Wood – The wood was intensively mined in the 18th century for limestone, used as flux in iron foundries. Nature has reclaimed the area which is now a delightful mix of woods, wetland and grassland. Remnants of canal wharf buildings, pit shafts and pump housings are still visible, scattered through the woods.

Barr Beacon – At 744 feet the Beacon is one of the highest points in the Midlands and offers marvellous views from the Black Country and Welsh Hills to Cannock Chase. The Beacon is the focal point of the Beacon Regional Park, a scattered area of dozens of open spaces. The Beacon Way and the park are managed by a partnership of Walsall, Sandwell and Birmingham councils and the Countryside Commission.

REFRESHMENTS:
None on the route. The nearest is *The Three Crowns* on the Sutton Road.

Walk 96 BROWNHILLS COMMON AND WYRLEY CANAL 9½m (15km)

Maps: OS Sheets Landranger 139; Pathfinder 892.

A fascinating long walk across a common and along canal towpaths. Excellent for wildlife enthusiasts.

Start: At 036072, Chasewater car park.

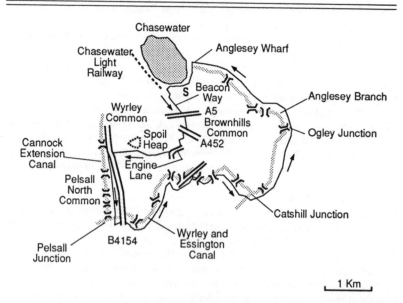

From the car park, turn left alongside Chasewater reservoir (*see* Note to Walk 6) following the Beacon Way (*see* Note to Walk 95). Go left again past the Chasewater Light Railway station. Now, by the bridge, go ahead over a stile to join the path along the dismantled railway. At its end, cross the A5, with care, to reach **Brownhills Common.** Follow the Beacon Way markers southwards across the common, then go right, over the old railway line, and down steps to reach the busy A452. Cross, with care, and continue along the Beacon Way, which is well defined as it traverses heathland and passes a pool to reach Engine Lane. Turn right, passing an industrial estate, and where the Beacon Way turns left, keep straight on along a bridleway. Ignore any paths to the right and keep fields to the left, eventually entering woods on the edge of Wyrley Common.

Follow the path running through the left edge of the wood (a spoil heap lies off to the right – the haunt of mountain bikes!). The path ends rather abruptly at the side of the very busy B4154. Cross this road, with great care, and turn right along the pavement. Just past the Littleoaks Kennels, take a path on the left which leads (through summer nettles!) to the towpath of the **Cannock Extension Canal**. Turn left along the towpath which runs straight as a die under five bridges and through Pelsall North Common, an area of rare heathland which is well worth exploring, to reach the Pelsall Junction. Go over the bridge to join the **Wyrley and Essington Canal**, rejoining the Beacon Way again for a short distance. Turn left along the towpath (with the canal on your left) and go under nine bridges to reach Catshill Junction. Cross the bridge and turn left up the towpath, crossing the Ogley Junction bridge on to the Anglesey Branch Canal. Follow this for almost three miles to its end at Anglesey Wharf. Now turn left along a lane to reach the starting car park.

POINTS OF INTEREST:

Brownhills Common – The Common comprises 100 acres of attractive lowland heathland. It was formerly part of Cannock Forest, which was felled during the 15th and 16th centuries. The Coppice Colliery once occupied the site, although little evidence of the Common's industrial past remains.

Cannock Extension Canal – The canal was constructed between 1858 and 1863 and was once connected to the Staffordshire and Worcester Canal. A canal basin served the Brownhills Colliery. The north section of the canal was closed in 1963 owing to subsidence.

Wyrley and Essington Canal – This was built in the 1790s before locks were invented. It was known as the Curley Wyrley because of the many twists and turns it executed through the countryside to maintain the same level.

REFRESHMENTS:

The Royal Oak, Yorks Bridge, Pelsall.
There is a cafe at the Chasewater Light Railway and a cafe/kiosk is open at peak times in Chasewater Park.

SHIPSTON-ON-STOUR

10m (16km)
or 12m (19$\frac{1}{2}$km)

Maps: OS Sheets Landranger 151; Pathfinder 1021 and 1044.
A long walk visiting four charming villages.
Start: At 258405, the High St/West St junction, Shipston.

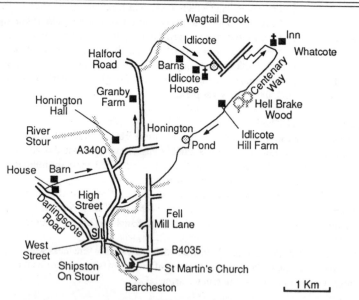

Walk up West Street, then go right up Darlingscote Road. After a mile, and just past
a house on the right, go through a gate on the right and walk past a barn. Keep a hedge
on your right across three fields to the A3400. Turn left, with care, then right over
Honington bridge into the village. Turn left into Halford Road. Walk past Granby
Farm and over a bridge by a wind pump. Turn right through a gate and follow Wagtail
Brook, across several fields, then cross a footbridge on the right. Follow a path uphill,
and on clearing trees, turn left passing to the left of the barns. Cross a track and
continue uphill, with a hedge on your left. Go through two gates, pass Idlicote House
and swing left by the church into **Idlicote**. Go past a pond and turn right down a road,
cutting the corner, left, across a field. Turn left along the road to reach barns on the
right. Go through a gate to the left of the barn, walk ahead, then go left over a stile.

Turn right, then left at a marker post. Follow a similar zigzag right and left to a bridge. Walk half-right, by telegraph poles, go through two kissing gates and turn right to the churchyard in **Whatcote**. Go through a gate in the top right corner to join the Centenary Way. Turn right beside the hedge, cross four fields and, just before Hell Brake Wood, turn right over a stile. Go left along the wood's edge, swinging right to a crossroads of tracks. Turn left along a tarmac lane and go left of Idlicote Hill Farm. Turn right, with the fence on your right, then switch sides of a hedge. Walk down a field and, just past a deer fence, turn left to the field end. Turn right (hedge on your right) across two fields. Go left at the corner and swing right past a pond, on the right. At the end, turn right, then left and right along a field edge, switching sides halfway. Keep the hedge on your right to reach a bridleway. Turn right, and immediately left over a stile, then head for the bottom right corner. Now head diagonally left across two fields to Fell Mill Lane. Turn left and cross a bridge.

The shorter route turns right to follow the Centenary Way, which is well waymarked across fields to the A3400. Turn left to reach Shipston.

The longer route follows the road for a mile. Cross the B4035, with care, and take the first right into **Barcheston**. Go past St Martin's Church, with its leaning tower, and at the lane's end, cross a stile on the right. Keep the river to your left and cross four fields to reach the B4035. Turn left into Shipston.

POINTS OF INTEREST:

Honington – The village once belonged to the Benedictine Priory of Coventry, passing, after the Dissolution, to the Gibbs family and, in 1668, to Sir Henry Parker. He built the five arch 17th-century bridge which was restored in the mid-1970s.

Idlicote – The estate belonged to the monks of Kenilworth until the Dissolution, when it was given to Thomas Cawarden, Master of the Revels to Henry VIII. It eventually passed to William Underhill, who sold New Place to William Shakespeare. Underhill was murdered by his son Fulke in 1597 and the manor was eventually rebuilt by Sir John Soane.

Whatcote – The south porch and nave wall of St Peter's Church were damaged by a bomb on 12th December 1940.

Barcheston – When William Willington purchased the village in 1507 he enclosed the land, evicting the tenants and effectively depopulating the village. In the 16th century William Sheldon made the famous tapestry maps of English counties here.

REFRESHMENTS:

The Royal Oak, Whatcote.

There are numerous possibilities in Shipston-on-Stour.

Walk 99   BIDFORD AND WELFORD   10m (16km)

Maps: OS Sheets Landranger 150 and 151; Pathfinder 997.

A long ramble near the River Avon, visiting four charming villages.

Start: At 099517, the Recreation Ground car park, Bidford.

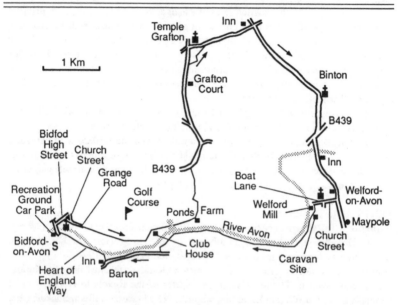

Turn left over the bridge (built, in 1482, at the spot where the Roman Icknield Street crossed the River Avon) and turn right up High Street. By the church, turn right down Church Street into Grange Road. Go over the cattle grid at the end and, at a sharp right bend, keep straight on beside the golf course. When the hedge on the left ends, continue ahead, following the well-marked path towards the buildings. The path turns left, then right along an enclosed path – little more than a muddy, overgrown ditch – skirting the clubhouse (presumably to keep riff-raff like walkers out of sight of the clubhouse windows!). By the car park, go straight ahead, with a hedge on your right, walking down the course and between ponds. Maintain direction to cross a stile in the top right corner of the course, then aim for the top left corner of a field and turn left in front of the barns to join a farm lane going left.

Turn left at a T-junction to reach the B439. Turn right and, shortly, left along a minor road to **Temple Grafton**. Keep right at a fork, passing Grafton Court to reach a stile on the right. Walk diagonally across fields to reach the village. Turn right and at the next crossroads, by the inn, turn right along the road into **Binton**. Ignore a left turn to Lower Binton, continuing along the road to reach the B439. Turn right and, shortly, left across a bridge. Continue past the inns into **Welford-on-Avon**.

If you want to see the maypole, keep straight on to the other end of the village. The route turns right down Church Street. Go past the church to the end of Boat Lane and take a narrow path on the left to reach another lane in front of Welford Mill. Turn left and, shortly, right through a caravan site to reach a stile in the top right corner. Go over on to a path between fences. The path crosses several fields, keeping close to the River Avon for two miles. Do not be tempted by any paths on the left, until you are just past the weir and lock and almost opposite the golf course. Now go over a footbridge and follow a lane away from the river to reach a minor road. Turn right into Barton. Where the road swings left by the inn, turn right over a stile to rejoin the riverside path. Go left across a flood barrier and over a stile into a field. The path (the Heart of England Way) now runs parallel to the river, crossing fields to reach the bridge and car park in **Bidford-on-Avon**.

POINTS OF INTEREST:

Temple Grafton – The village is so called because in the reign of Henry III, the Knights Templar built a church here. The old church was replaced in 1875 by the present unusual building.

Binton – St Peter's Church is famous for its memorial west window to Captain Robert Falcon Scott. His wife Kathleen was the rector's sister. The window, paid for by public subscription and unveiled in 1915, shows the attempt on the South Pole.

Welford-on-Avon – A beautiful village with many attractive thatched cottages. The striking 65 foot maypole possibly dates from the 14th century. The original, Saxon, Church of St Peter was built by the Priory of Deerhurst and has a much photographed timber-framed, lych gate.

Bidford-on-Avon – This was a Saxon settlement originally called Bydas Ford. An Anglo-Saxon burial ground discovered here in 1922 yielded many fine artefacts.

REFRESHMENTS:

The Four Alls Inn, Welford-on-Avon.
The Cottage of Content, Barton.
The Blue Boar, Temple Grafton.
There are also several fine inns and an excellent bakery/tea shop in Bidford-on-Avon.

Walk 100   SHUCKBURGH AND FLECKNOE   12m (19$\frac{1}{2}$km)
Maps: OS Sheets Landranger 151; Pathfinder 977.
*A Figure of Eight with a long stretch of canal, gated lanes and
delightful parkland.*
Start: At 492628, the canal bridge, Lower Shuckburgh.

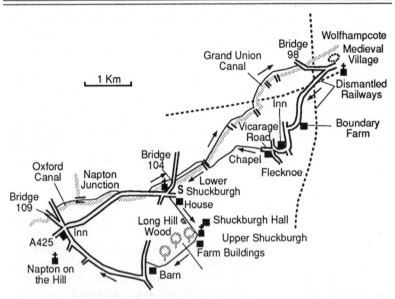

Cars may be parked by the canal bridge but please do not obstruct the gateway.

From Bridge 104, turn right up the towpath of the Grand Union Canal for 3 miles,
passing 5 bridges, including a dismantled bridge of the old LNWR railway. At the 6th
bridge, No. 98, turn right along a lane into **Wolfhampcote**, crossing a bridge over the
old Great Central Railway. The church lies straight ahead at the T-junction, but the
route turns right down the gated road. After a short distance, recross the old railways,
go past Boundary Farm and turn left at a T-junction to swing right into **Flecknoe**.

Ignore a left turn and keep ahead, passing the inn to reach a junction. Turn left,
then right by the chapel to go down Vicarage Road. Go through a gate at the end and
straight across a field. Go through the hedgerow and along the left edge of the field to
reach a gap halfway along. Turn left and walk across fields to reach a canal bridge.

Cross and turn left along a bridleway, parallel to the canal, going through several gates to reach Bridge 104. Turn left (passing the start) and walk past St John the Baptist Church in Lower Shuckburgh. Cross the A425, with care, and climb the stile opposite. Go half-left, through two gates, passing to the right of a house with three chimneys. Go over a culvert and turn left, uphill, walking parallel to telegraph poles. Cross a stile and go through a kissing gate, heading towards a gap on the skyline to reach a gate into Shuckburgh Park. As notices remind you, dogs should be on a lead and all gates closed. Also, no access is allowed to the rest of the park beyond the public footpaths.

Continue until you see farm buildings, with the church of **Upper Shuckburgh** hidden in trees on the left. Beyond is Shuckburgh Hall – not open to the public. Do not pass the farm: instead, turn right through a gate and follow the edge of Long Hill Wood, going through several gateways. On reaching the end of the wood, turn right and descend the slope past a brick barn. Cross two stiles and a footbridge, then turn left across a field to a lane. Turn left, through a gate, to reach a T-junction and turn right into Napton on the Hill. Now ignore a left turn and turn right at the T-junction. Go down the hill and straight over the A425 crossroads, with care, to reach Bridge 109 on the Oxford Canal. Turn right along the towpath, passing Napton Junction where the Grand Union Canal joins. Continue along the towpath to reach Bridge 104 and the start.

POINTS OF INTEREST:

Wolfhampcote – Opposite the church are the remains of a village abandoned in the late 15th century after forced eviction of the tenants by landowners who wanted the land for sheep. The site was excavated in 1955 when over 2,000 items were discovered including pottery, knives, buckles and a barrel padlock, one of only four found in this country. St Peter's Church, now in the care of the Redundant Churches Fund, has a 14th-century south aisle with a three-bay arcade, a 14th-century north chapel and a heavily restored chancel.

Flecknoe – This attractive village, on the slopes of Bush Hill, has the old stocks outside its Post Office.

Upper Shuckburgh – Only ridges and furrows remain of a deserted village. The Hall has been the home of the Shuckburgh family since the 11th century: the present house was built in 1844 in front of an older timber-framed building. St John in the Wilderness Church contains brasses and monuments to the Shuckburgh family.

REFRESHMENTS:

The King's Head, Napton on the Hill.
The Old Olive Bush, Flecknoe.